Praise for Russ Hedge &
"Life Happens… and Then You Choose!"

"Life happens…and for some it happens in the wrong direction - all the bad. But…we have the ability to choose - we can make choices. Choose to read these beautiful words and pages from Russ to separate your thoughts by the power of faith and positivity. Smile - you have the ability to smile through such challenges and hardships - finding joy and happiness in the most life changing circumstances - let Russ be the tour guide."
–Michael Ray, Smile Project Louisville

"In *Life Happens… and then you Choose,* Russ Hedge has written an impactful and persuasive book that reminds us we always have a choice in how we respond to life's challenges. Blending Scripture, poetry, quotes, and personal stories— including his battle with cancer, a devastating car accident, and family connections – Russ offers proven advice on how to turn pain into purpose. This is an encouraging and motivating book filled with hope for anyone seeking to grow in faith, overcome fear and limiting beliefs, and discover meaning through adversity."
–Terry Tucker is a motivational speaker, cancer warrior, and author of Sustainable Excellence and 4 Truths and a Lie.

"This book 'Life Happens…and Then You Choose' contains the greatest collection of brilliant Scriptures, Quotes and Wisdom; woven into an incredible Journey of Challenges overcome by Russ Hedge. Russ chose to live the life he has now. Which is; to be the best example of how faith in God, a positive attitude, being grateful and a belief in yourself will help influence so many others in conquering their own life challenges."
–Fred Kienle "The Attitude Guru" is an Author, Speaker and Entertainer

"I often refer to Russ Hedge as the walking New Testament and character personified. If you want to work with someone who is not only an expert in his industry, but also a man of unmatched love and care for people, Russ is your guy. Every single day, even while battling cancer, he rises to inspire and serve others. That level of courage and consistency is rare. Russ isn't just talking about living a purpose-driven life, he *is* the living definition."
–Mike Ashabraner The Redneck Connector, Founder, Hounds of Business Community

"Inspiring! Russ Hedge lives the wisdom he shares in "*Life Happens...and Then You Choose*". Through his powerful story of faith, resilience, and courage in the face of life's toughest trials, this book becomes a true guide for anyone seeking hope and strength. It's an inspiring reminder that no matter the obstacles, we can choose to live with passion, purpose, and persistence, and create an extraordinary life and pay that forward."
–Lisa Marree - Scientist | Holistic Menopause Specialist

I have the privilege of calling Russ a friend and co-host for many years. What I value most is the consistency of his message: life will happen, but how you respond is up to you. "Life Happens and Then You Choose" captures his voice perfectly - it's inspirational, uplifting, and practical. If you've ever wanted Russ cheering you on in your daily life, this book delivers exactly that.

–D. Scott Smith - Radio Host, Author, and Motivational Listener

Russ tells it like it is, AND like it can be - even in the midst of reality. You will see your own life on many pages in this book. You'll also see Russ's practical guidance for navigating life-threatening illness, personal loss, grief, and more in ways that do not merely get you through but actually make those seasons count. He helps you see this is do-able. If you're facing challenges and wondering if joy is still possible, sit with Russ while he tells you his story. Follow his coaching, and you won't be the same at the end.

–Rev. Debbie Lamm Bray, PhD, Associate Director for Educational Programs, COEE Team, Northwest University

Russ Hedge
Inspirational Speaker

Inspiration and Motivation

Russ Hedge is an Inspirational Speaker, Marketing Coach, Livestream Producer. He is available for in person or virtual speaking engagements. Russ believes... An inspired and encouraged team is a productive team. So let him help yours today.

For more information on how to book Russ to speak, or take advantage of his marketing coaching, and livestream producing, go to...

RussHedge.com or email him at russ@russhedge.com

LIFE HAPPENS...
AND THEN YOU
CHOOSE!

RUSS HEDGE

Printed in the United States of America

First Printing 2025

ISBN: 979-8-9935101-1-8

Adriel Publishing

Cover design by Everlie Mortillero

Photographs by Miriam Haugen of Haugen's Galleri

Edited by my amazing family and community

russ@russhedge.com

Dedicated to…

My beautiful wife, Leah, and to my amazing children, Kyla and Connor, along with my wonderful daughter-in-law, Gabby. You are my greatest blessing, my inspiration, and my daily joy. God has truly given me an incredible support system, and I dedicate this book to you. I love you all so much. My life is better because of you.

CONTENTS

INTRODUCTION

LIFE HAPPENS

For a moment, my heart seemed to stop… What began on my foot had now traveled all the way to my brain. My Radiation Oncologist explained that the MRI showed a tumor in the left temporal lobe.

Life is a battle to be won. From the moment you wake up, the battle begins—both within you and all around you. The question is: How will you fight?

Will you rise up with faith and purpose, choosing a positive, Godly perspective? Or will you surrender and let negativity claim the victory?
Every single day, the choice is yours.
Be bold. Stand firm.

Life happens… and then you choose!

"Do not be conformed to this world, but be transformed by the renewing of your mind…"
—Romans 12:2 (ESV)

So ask yourself…

What perspective will you start your day with?

What kind of mindset will you embrace?

DON'T BELIEVE THE LIES

Don't believe the lies and negative thoughts that often sneak in and overtake your thinking first thing in the morning. You get to choose your thoughts. Just like life, **they happen… and you choose**. You get to filter through them and choose what deserves your focus.

BE PROACTIVE

Better yet – **be proactive**.

Start filling your mind with **positive Godly thoughts** the very moment you wake up.

I do this every day: I choose my thoughts before my feet even hit the floor. I decide in advance what kind of day I am going to have.

It can be challenging. Negative thoughts may beat you to the punch and start the day's movie trailer before you get a chance to take control, but you don't have to give the negative thoughts power over you.

This is where my theme of life begins…

Life Happens… and Then You Choose!

ABOUT ME... YOUR AUTHOR

I am a Christ-follower, blessed to be married to my beautiful wife, Leah for almost 38 years. Together, we have two amazing adult children, Kyla and Connor, and a wonderful daughter-in-law, Gabby.

I was very fortunate growing up. I had a blessed childhood with loving, supportive parents. I was raised in a safe environment filled with incredible opportunities. But as many of us know, life can change quickly.

Despite the blessings of my early years, life began to shift as I entered adulthood. After a very successful high school experience, I went off to college—and that's when the real challenges began.

College brought a whole new environment, and it felt like the rules had suddenly changed. Can you relate? Have you ever found yourself in a season where the lines between right and wrong seemed to blur?

At Oregon State University, I stepped into adulthood and had to start making decisions on my own. My parents were no longer part of my daily routine, and I was living independently for the first time.

Unfortunately, I made some poor choices. I found myself struggling to navigate this new life and just keep my head above water.

Then, the summer of 1983, after my first year, I was in a near-fatal car accident. By God's grace, I survived. I returned to college and continued on, again making my own choices, and still struggling.

I was truly blessed. Without even realizing it, God was guiding my steps, and in that journey, I met an incredibly beautiful woman who would become my wife. I surrendered my life to Jesus, and together we built a beautiful family. For the first time, since college began, it felt like life was moving in the right direction.

But as the years went by and our children grew into adulthood, I faced new challenges—this time with my parents. I walked through the difficult seasons of cancer, dementia, and Alzheimer's with them. It was hard, but it also was a blessing in disguise as I spent many precious hours with them in their final years. And after both of them passed on to Heaven, I received my own diagnosis… cancer! My diagnosis progressed quickly, from Stage 2A to 3C, and eventually to Stage 4.

These seasons of hardship made life increasingly difficult. Every step required intentional choices. But through it all, I came to understand something powerful—with God's help, I still had to choose the right perspective daily.

As I shared in my first book, **Befuddled? Live the Life You Choose!**, I realized that no matter what happened around me, I still had a choice. Life didn't stop happening—but I had a say in how I responded. And in the middle of all the chaos, pain, and uncertainty, I began to recognize something profound: I was truly blessed. In fact, there were far more good and positive things in my life than bad—I just had to choose where to place my focus.

Would I focus on the negative, or would I focus on the positive?

When I stepped back and took stock, the truth became clear. The good outweighed the bad. I was deeply blessed—even in the middle of it all.

So now, I'm here to encourage you. Life will continue to happen. But always remember this:

Life happens… and then you choose.

1 - LIFE HAPPENS... AND THEN YOU CHOOSE!

I Have Cancer?

My mind reeled with my doctor's words. *Am I going to die and leave my family so soon?*

Every single day, ***"Life Happens… and Then You Choose!"***

Things happen in life that you never planned, and suddenly you're forced to navigate challenges you never expected.

I never planned to get cancer—but I did. That diagnosis changed not only my perspective, but also the entire rhythm of my life.

Everything began happening so rapidly, and I had to make choices based on the perspective I had in the middle of those circumstances.

Being a strong man of faith, I knew God was with me in the midst of my diagnosis. I could feel His strength and peace holding me up, yet it was still a lot to take in. I was scared—overwhelmed, to say the least. But after the initial shock, I became determined to keep a good perspective.

"Today I have given you the choice between life and death, between blessings and curses... Oh, that you would choose life." —Deuteronomy 30:19

Life is not always easy. Believe me when I say this has been no simple journey. Yes, I trust God, but it can still feel overwhelming and hard to navigate. Even so, I keep moving forward—one step at a time.

STOP AND EVALUATE

As I will begin to talk about in the next chapter, I have had several life-changing experiences that have made me stop and evaluate my life and my faith. Even when you are a positive and optimistic person like me, you still have problems. There are still circumstances that shake your faith. I have been faced with life and death and have come out the other side, trusting that God has a good plan through it all. Even when the circumstances I have faced have been anything but good.

No one gets a free pass. Jesus said in John 16:33, *"I have told you all this so that you may have peace in me. Here on earth you will have many trials and sorrows. But take heart, because I have overcome the world."*

Well, that is good news, since I have not had the strength on my own to overcome the things that have happened to me. I believe we all need something much bigger than ourselves to help us through the storms of life. We need that peace that passes all understanding.

THRIVE, NOT JUST SURVIVE

No matter what you are going through, you can make it. You can overcome your circumstances with God's help and make a choice to thrive, not just survive.

Make the most of every moment.

You get one shot at this life on earth because… **time is non-refundable, so give it all you've got!**

Life is constantly changing and we are transforming into who God created us to be.

It's a journey.

"Transformation is a process, and as life happens there are tons of ups and downs. It's a journey of discovery - there are moments on mountaintops and moments in deep valleys of despair." —Rick Warren

DON'T LET FEAR WIN

So often fear tries to stop us. Our limiting beliefs and imposter syndrome creep in and threaten to put on the brakes. But remember, God has a reason and a purpose for your life.

Through my journey, things started piling up, and still are to some degree. It is often overwhelming, but I truly believe **"*I can do all things through Christ who gives me strength.*"** —Philippians 4:13 (NIV)

Just when I think I can't go on, Jesus is there with that peace that surpasses all understanding. His still, quiet voice reminds me that it's going to be okay. He's got this. So, when fear and problems start piling up, I take a deep breath and remember that I am more than a conqueror. Life offers so much to learn and grow from; we just need to be present and pay attention.

Adversity is definitely the best teacher, if we allow ourselves to experience and learn from what is happening.

Judith Durham says, *"Everything in life happens for a reason and it's important to embrace it."* Embrace it and choose; Choose where to go next and what to do with your life circumstances.

Just remember, *"Life happens… and then you choose!"*

Even through life's struggles, you get to choose.

Deuteronomy 30:19 continues on and says, *"Now I call on heaven and earth to witness the choice you make. Oh, that you would choose life, so that you and your descendants might live!"*

I love it… And I choose life.

When life takes you by surprise and your road is a bit crooked, pause, take a look at what's ahead, and just take the next step.

Remember, as Martin Luther King Jr. said, *"You don't have to see the whole staircase, just the first step."*

FIRST STEP

So choose to take that first step. That is where the journey begins. Choose to be authentic and uniquely you. Be yourself. Choose to live life to the fullest and let God show you your path. After all, He is the one who gives you free choice.

Trust Him.

"Trust in the Lord with all your heart; do not depend on your own understanding. Seek his will in all you do, and he will show you which path to take." —Proverbs 3:5-6

If you ask me… That's a good choice.

So as life happens, don't let yourself get discouraged and let fears overtake your life.

We really only have two main directions to choose. We can head in a positive direction, or a negative one. It is as simple as that. But, it's not easy.

YOU CAN DO IT

You have to intentionally choose.

So choose wisely.

And don't forget to keep a positive mindset and a good perspective.

Keep moving forward and don't let fear stop you!

Remember...

"Life Happens... and Then You Choose!"

2 - OVERCOMING FEARS & CHALLENGES

(Adapted from my chapter in the International Best Selling, "Beyond Boundaries")

How do you overcome your fears & challenges when life brings unwelcome surprises?

How do you thrive in an environment where survival is the human instinct?

MINDSET AND PERSPECTIVE

The answer lies in your mindset and perspective. I believe that with God, all things are possible. As Isaiah 41:10 declares, *"Don't be afraid, for I am with you. Don't be discouraged, for I am your God. I will strengthen you and help you. I will hold you up with my victorious right hand."* That truth changes everything—your focus, your courage, and your ability to move forward in faith.

I have learned that even with God's help, it takes one step at a time, slow and steady progress, working through fear and failures.

Jeanette Coron says, ***"Don't let your fear of failure keep you away from your destiny."***

I believe I was created to do something amazing, and I get to choose my path each day.

I love a poem I learned years ago, ***"The Road, Not Taken"*** by Robert Frost.

"Two roads diverged in a yellow wood,
And sorry I could not travel both
And be one traveler, long I stood
And looked down one as far as I could
To where it bent in the undergrowth;

Then took the other, as just as fair,
And having perhaps the better claim,
Because it was grassy and wanted wear;
Though as for that the passing there
Had worn them really about the same,

And both that morning equally lay
In leaves no step had trodden black.
Oh, I kept the first for another day!

Yet knowing how way leads on to way,
I doubted if I should ever come back.

I shall be telling this with a sigh
Somewhere ages and ages hence:
Two roads diverged in a wood, and I—
I took the one less traveled by,
And that has made all the difference."

CHOICES

The main theme of this poem is *choices.* We all have
the God-given ability to choose our path.

We are not called to live exactly like everyone else.
God created each of us to be unique, and the path
He sets before us is just as unique.
Every day… ***"Life happens, and then you choose!"***

My own journey has been filled with struggles,
challenges, and countless decisions—each one
shaping the person I am today.

And that is where my story begins…

61 YEAR JOURNEY

I recently turned 61 years young. I have had a blessed life, but it has definitely not always been easy. I learned early on, whatever my circumstances, to continue to show up and put one foot in front of the other, no matter what is thrown at me.

And I work hard, not to let my fears stop me.

"Fear kills more dreams than failure ever will." - Unknown

I've learned to muster up courage, with God's help, even when it's hard.

"Courage is not the absence of fear, but rather the assessment that something else is more important than fear." —Franklin D. Roosevelt

FACE YOUR FEARS

I remember one of the first big moments in my life when I had to face fear and muster some real courage. I was in high school, playing football, and it happened during summer practice before the season officially began.

I don't remember exactly how it all started, but suddenly, I found myself in the middle of one of those classic playground-style fights—the kind where a crowd quickly forms a circle and starts cheering.

The problem was... I was the one in the center of the circle.

Now let me tell you, I am really a lover, not a fighter, but here I was fighting one of my teammates, who had been the Alaska Boxing Champion in his age group just a few years earlier.

Before I knew it, he punched me in the face. This was more than a little startling. I was bigger than him, but he was quicker than me. Because of my size advantage, I went to my classic headlock move my dad had taught me. This definitely stopped the punches, and I took control of the situation. After having him in the headlock for a while, I was pulled off by another teammate, and I left the group running. In fact, I ran about 5 miles, all the way home.

I was scheduled to go back to football practice that night, and I really didn't want to go. I remember my dad saying, **"Son, you have to face your fears."** So back I went—and to my surprise, there were no further problems. I had faced my fears, and everything turned out okay. In fact, as time went on, I even became good friends with the teammate I had fought with.

Author Bob Goff says, **"We all encounter difficulties. It's what we do next that defines us."**

That moment taught me an important lesson: to face my fears and refuse to let them hold me back. Life has brought challenges and even serious health issues, but I've learned that with faith and courage, you can keep moving forward no matter what comes your way.

So what happens when you are thrust into some major life challenges. Do you just survive, or do you fight for life and thrive?

Challenges will come and how you deal with them determines how you will spend the rest of your life.

It's up to you.

3 - LIFE CAN CHANGE IN AN INSTANT

(Adapted from my chapter in the International Best-Selling, "Beyond Boundaries")

It was July 9th, 1983. I had just finished my freshman year at Oregon State University.

It was a sunny summer day, and I was working with my dad in his new satellite TV business. We were installing a satellite dish and struggling with the challenges we were facing—and, in turn, frustrated with each other. I decided to take a break.

I drove to a nearby golf course to play nine holes. I just needed to relax.

To this day, I don't remember leaving the golf course and driving home. I was in my used—but new to me —Toyota Celica, which I had owned for only seven days. As I entered Highway 99E in Canby, Oregon, I was struck by a truck traveling about 60 miles per hour and thrown into a tree next to a church called New Life.

First responders quickly called LifeFlight and closed down the highway so the helicopter could land. I was extracted from my car using the Jaws of Life and flown to Emanuel Hospital in Portland, Oregon.

A surgical trauma team was waiting for me. I had brain trauma and swelling, a punctured lung, both lungs collapsed, broken collarbones, a broken jaw, broken ribs, and third-degree burns on my feet. I was badly injured—but by the grace of God, I was holding on to life. I am a fighter. After surgery, I spent almost four weeks in the hospital. I have no memory of the first two and a half weeks of my stay—but honestly, that was a blessing in disguise. Through the worst part of my recovery, God took away the memory of my pain.

My amazing parents and sister were with me every step of the way. In early August, I was finally sent home, and even through the trauma to my body, I was determined to rehab and return to Oregon State University for my sophomore year. The doctors didn't believe I could do it—but with God's help, strength, and my resilience, I was back at OSU that fall.

I've learned that through life's struggles, we don't have to stay stuck. We can move forward with determination and grit to create a better life. Whether it's a physical challenge or an emotional one, we have the power to choose to push through and come out stronger on the other side.

So wherever you are, don't live in your negative circumstances. Break free and live with a positive mindset and perspective—no matter what you are going through.

As C.C. Scott wisely said, *"The human spirit is stronger than anything that can happen to it."*

And my journey continued...

LIFE IS ALWAYS CHANGING... SO IS YOUR ROLE

My parents have always been amazing. They were my role models and my heroes. After years of their love and support, their health began to fail. They had taken care of me for so many years, and now it was my turn.

After being a lifelong smoker, my dad battled lung cancer. Following a major surgery, he almost didn't make it. He had to have nearly one lung removed and struggled to recover, but he rebounded for a few years. Eventually, his health began to fail again—he became unsteady and frail.

My mama had been diagnosed with Alzheimer's and was struggling with her memory. I had to make a choice and step in to help guide the process.

With the help of my beautiful wife, Leah, we sold their home and moved them to a nice retirement community. Unfortunately, despite our efforts, my dad only had a few months left. After a steady decline, he lost his battle with cancer.

I remember the last couple of days vividly. Dad was already in hospice, and things were not looking good. With the encouragement of Leah, I spent the night with my parents in their apartment. Our part-time caregiver was out of town, and things were difficult. After a rough night, I knew something had to change. The next day, I hired a full-time caregiver and called the hospice nurse—Dad was in a lot of pain. Watching my hero suffer was almost more than I could bear. The nurse administered his pain medication, and I prayed. It felt like hours before he finally settled, but at last, he rested peacefully.

I remember it like it was yesterday. He called for my mama, and she came and laid down next to him on their bed. They held hands, and he said, "I love you, Mama." She replied, "I love you, Papa," and they fell asleep. I told the caregiver I was exhausted and needed a few hours of rest in my own bed, but I would be back early the next morning. I left just after 11 p.m. and received a call around 1 a.m. that he had stopped breathing and had gone to be with the Lord.

It was a tough last day, but I am so thankful for the beautiful memory of my parents loving each other and ending their married journey together in peace.

Through this, I learned the importance of making lasting memories, intentionally. How we live every moment is so important.

As Leo Buscaglia said, *"Too often we underestimate the power of a touch, a smile, a kind word, a listening ear, an honest compliment, or the smallest act of caring, all of which have the potential to turn a life around."*

BE PRESENT AND CHOOSE LIFE

Live each moment by being present. Choose to thrive, not just survive.

I spent the next couple years loving Mama, and enjoying the happy moments. We had so many happy moments that I chose to record many of them. We enjoyed what I called **#HappyMomentsWithMama**. We would walk, laugh, and sing, doing laps around her memory care hallway. She called it **#LapinAndLaughin**. I shared much of this journey with my community on social media. It inspired so many through the joy my mama had, even through her last couple years of life.

I cherished those moments and created memories I will carry forever. On July 18th, 2022—my dad's birthday—I lost Mama. That day, she joined him in heaven and shared in his celebration.

YOU CHOOSE YOUR PERSPECTIVE

Your perspective is up to you! With intention and courage, you can do the amazing things God created you to do.

It is easy to get discouraged when you stumble along the way, but that is inevitable, because you are human.

But you don't have to just survive, you can thrive! In scripture, God says, ***"Don't be afraid, for I am with you. Don't be discouraged, for I am your God!"*** —Isaiah 41:10

There is something bigger than all of us, and when you lean into that strength, the impossible becomes possible.

BE A DIFFERENCE MAKER

Choose to be a world-changer and a difference-maker, even if your circumstances tell you otherwise. Through health challenges or car accidents, fights or disappointments, you can find your way through.

You can thrive your way through! So why not start today!

4 - PERSPECTIVES ON CANCER

(Adapted from my Chapter in "Perspectives on Cancer" Vol 2)

Perspective is everything when you are facing the challenges of life." —Joni Eareckson Tada

When I first heard the words, "You have cancer," it was shocking. My initial reaction was, "*No, not me. I'm the one who supports others through cancer—I never expected to face it myself.*"

I was blessed, God has given me a good perspective on life and a positive mindset, which definitely helped. But even the most positive person doesn't want to hear those words.

I had been a supporter of others with cancer and specifically, **"Showing Up: Perspectives on Cancer"** and **"Kickin Cancer,"** supporting others and their families battling cancer. It was not a journey I wanted to be on, but here I was.

DEALING WITH MY DIAGNOSIS

Although I was dealing with a different kind of cancer, it was still life threatening and a lot to deal with over the next year and a half. In fact, like I said, I have learned that cancer is a lifelong journey—one I am still dealing with today.

My life as an Inspiration Specialist was now being put to the test. I had to reshape my perspective based on my new circumstances.

I truly believe what Dani Johnson says *"You're not defined by your circumstances; you're defined by how you react to those circumstances."*

It is true… *"Life Happens, and Then You Choose!"*

I had to make a choice. What was my next step after finding out life-altering information? Was I going to give in, or move forward with my positive perspective?

It was definitely a defining moment.

THE STRENGTH OF FAITH

I am a man of faith, and God has continued to keep me strong in all circumstances in my life, so why not now?

But it's not always that easy. How we react makes a big difference.

"Life is 10% what happens to you and 90% how you react to it." —Charles R. Swindoll

CANCER JOURNEY

It was July of 2022 when I discovered what turned out to be cancer on the bottom of my foot, stage 2A invasive Melanoma.

The "C" word was alarming but the way the dermatologist described it, it sounded fairly routine. I thought, "No big deal, they will cut out the cancer and I'll be all good."

Because of my God-given perspective on life, I usually just roll with the punches. ***"It's all good"*** is my motto!

Like I said earlier, perspective is everything when you are facing life threatening circumstances.

It is so much easier to have a positive perspective when life is good. It's when the challenges come that the rubber meets the road. It's how you bounce back after you fall down that matters.

"It's not how far you fall, but how high you bounce that counts." —Zig Ziglar

After being referred to Oregon Health Sciences University (OHSU) to see an oncologist the reality really began to set in.

I had surgery on November 11th, 2022.

We were all feeling optimistic.

A few days later, I opened my email. I saw an OHSU MyChart Message with the test results from pathology. I was expecting more good news.

As I wrote in chapter 2, the news was not what I had expected and they found more cancer. I was at Stage 3C now and further treatment or surgery was needed.

The news really shook me and my family. In fact, my son and daughter-in-law called from California to find out the results and as I began to tell them, I looked up at my wife and daughter, both with tears running down their faces, and I lost it. I couldn't talk. It was a life changing moment.

I always look for the positive, and this was difficult, but God was going to use this experience to grow and guide me. He was going to help me to encourage thousands of people.

It was a pivotal moment, and one that took most of the night to recover from. But tomorrow was coming.

TOMORROW IS A NEW DAY

My dad, my hero, used to always say, ***"Tomorrow's a new day!"*** After a good night's sleep, the morning brings a fresh perspective.

I truly believe we have to experience the emotions of each situation, but as the saying goes, time heals all wounds, and I knew I was going to grow through this experience and come out better on the other side.

I love the quote by Justin Winski, *"Don't let your circumstances define you. You define your circumstances."*

It is only God and each of us that define who we are and what we are planning to do with our circumstances. We have to be intentional in our life.

After the initial shock of the diagnosis, I felt God saying to me, "It is going to be ok. I've got this!" I knew God was not done with me yet. I had a peace about the cancer, but knew I had more to do.

I truly live to Inspire and encourage others and this cancer in my life would define all I said and did from this point on.

I truly believe, **Life Happens… and Then You Choose**!

PURPOSE-DRIVEN

My "why" or purpose came alive. I believe I am here to *inspire and encourage others to live a purpose-driven life of significance*. To help people make a life changing impact and a difference now!

"A life is not important except in the impact it has on other lives." —Jackie Robinson

What is your impact on the lives of others?

What are you intentionally doing every day to make a difference and be a blessing to your fellow man?

"In every day, there are 1,440 minutes. That means we have 1,440 daily opportunities to make a positive impact." —Les Brown

That is amazing, and a lot of opportunities, most of us pass up daily. So you and I get to choose our path; the life we want to live.

BEFUDDLED

In 2020, at the height of COVID, I wrote and released my first book, *Befuddled? Live the Life You Choose!* It was a book about living with purpose and a positive mindset, in spite of life's circumstances. I talked about perspective and how you look at life… especially through life's challenging circumstances.

I have had some big moments happen over my lifetime. I wrote about my near fatal car accident in July of 1983 when I was only 19. I've lost both my parents: my dad to lung cancer and Mama to Alzheimer's. All of this happened in the month of July, coincidentally the same month I found what we thought was a wart on the bottom of my foot.

Even though I lived through challenges, this was different. This really shook me to the core. A life-threatening, unbelievable disease was actually happening to me.

RATTLED AWAKE

I first wrote about this journey in, *Rattled Awake*, volume one. That was an amazing opportunity, like this one for Perspectives on cancer, to collaborate with other authors and put together a book that will positively impact others.

My job as an Inspirational Speaker, Marketing Coach, Livestreamer, and Livestream Producer, gives me many opportunities to speak to people. Whether it is online, in person events, or through my writing, I am blessed to have the opportunity to speak into others' lives.

I want to be real in my communication as I feel authenticity is so important. My friend Nancy Debra Barrows would say, it was time to start #RadiatingReal.

I am blessed to be friends with Tim Sohn, the creator of the Showing Up: Perspectives on Cancer nonprofit. Over the past three years, I have been able to attend and speak at the yearly live conference. What an amazing opportunity to be with cancer warriors, caregivers, and supporters of the cause.

Any chance I have to impact others in a positive way, I'm all in. I continue to feel God using me to share my journey while displaying my positive attitude and perspective.

I try to always be honest and vulnerable and share how I am moving forward, even through ongoing challenges. It is not easy at times, but it is an intentional choice I make each day!

CONTINUED CHALLENGES

Truth is, the challenges kept coming. After the first round of Immunotherapy, they found more cancer in the lymph nodes in my right groin. I had to choose to change drugs in my treatment, or surgery. After speaking with my Oncologists and a weekend of prayer, I chose treatment.

My body didn't react well to the second treatment. I got extremely sick and developed Type 1 Diabetes as my pancreas started to shut down.

I had to have another surgery to remove more cancer. It was an invasive surgery and they removed 11 lymph nodes in my upper right groin area as well as moving a muscle to protect that area.

Once again a long recovery, but with a great result.

About a week and a half after the surgery, the pathology results came back and they found cancer only in one of the inflamed lymph nodes and it was contained. They had removed all the cancer.

They had planned to do radiation after the surgery, but the OHSU Tumor Board met and reviewed my situation and decided no more treatment was needed because I was cancer free.

My story is ongoing, and I intend to keep encouraging and inspiring others through my actions. I am believing for God's complete healing, but at this point I am having to adjust my rhythm of life to deal with the diabetes.

I am also dealing with additional things the trauma of cancer caused in my body. I have internal digestive issues, and after many procedures and tests they believe it is from colitis. For a while I was taking enzymes they thought my pancreas was not providing for my digestion. I also have had vertigo-like symptoms, hearing and vision problems.

Cancer is a lot for your body to take, but whether I deal with this temporarily or for a lifetime, I will continue to stay positive and keep a good perspective, knowing God has blessed me far beyond my problems and challenges.

As the amazing singer *Nightbirde* said, ***"I am so much more than my problems."***

Our story never ends, and the perspective we embrace will make a significant difference.

Today is the day you decide whether to live or not. It is your perspective that will drive you or stop you.

It's your choice.

5 - GOD'S NOT DONE WITH ME YET

It was August of 2024. Life stopped—just for a moment—when I got the pathology report. The cancer was back. And this time, it was stage 4. It had metastasized to my lungs and brain.

I sat quietly with my beautiful wife as my oncologist explained the challenges ahead, letting each word sink in. It would take time to absorb it all.

Then I remembered what my dad used to say: *"Tomorrow is a new day."*

So that's what I clung to. I went to bed, got a good night's sleep, and woke up with a fresh perspective.

Deep in my heart, I knew—God was not done with me yet. He had already used me in powerful ways, and I believed He still had more to do through me. The fight wasn't over. It was simply a new chapter.

WHAT'S AHEAD

I had more treatment ahead of me and life was looking more fragile all the time.

Through the toughest times, I know God is with me. He guides my footsteps. Even when I don't know where to go, I remember Proverbs 3:5-6 that says… *"Trust in the Lord with all your heart and do not depend on your own understanding. Seek His will in all you do, and He will show you what path to take."*

God gave me the peace that passes all understanding and showed me the path I was to take.

I knew He was not done with me yet.
There is so much opportunity still ahead.

HOPE

John Maxwell says *"Where there is no hope in the future, there is no power in the present."*
Hope brings power to achieve now and live our best life. It renews our spirit and gives us a reason to live.

Life is really amazing and we have power from our God. We have hope for a better today and a brighter tomorrow.

61 YEAR PERSPECTIVE

As I write this book, I reflect on my 61 years of life. Overall, in spite of my health challenges, I feel good… Thankful and blessed—and honestly, it's hard to believe I'm actually 61.

I definitely have my bumps in the road, but I have a renewed perspective on what is possible.

If you're like me, when you were young you thought your grandparents, at 60, were almost at the end of their life. Do you remember those days?

Now however, I have a different perspective being there myself and feeling like I have a lot of life left in me. I believe, even through the challenges, I can do so much more. Each day, I have renewed hope and believe God's not done with me yet!

"I can do all things through Christ who gives me strength." —Philippians 4:13

I am hopeful for the future and looking forward to this chapter of my life, filled with opportunities and abundance.

I serve an abundant God and the challenges I have had to go through have only made me stronger and opened up new doors to reach out to others. I know God is with me and this gives me strength.

FAITH

Being a strong man of faith, I truly believe Exodus 33:14, *"My Presence will go with you, and I will give you rest."*

God will give me the strength, peace, and rest I need. I have so many people to still inspire and encourage.

"Now faith is confidence in what we hope for and assurance about what we do not see."
—Hebrews 11:1 (NIV)

There is so much more than I can see; so much more that God has for me.

Even when I don't feel ready.

PURPOSE

As I said previously, my purpose in life is to ***Inspire and encourage you so you can live a purpose-driven life of significance.*** I want you to be a world changer—a difference maker. That is why God put me on this earth.

My purpose drives me every day to help others. Through the passing of my parents and my own cancer battle, I have had the opportunity to encourage and inspire people all over the world.

I believe I still have a long way to go, and I will keep taking one step after another—impacting my world for the good.

I know you have a God-given purpose too. Have you defined your purpose? You cannot implement a purpose you cannot define.

So... what is your purpose?

I have now lived over 61 years of life, I have developed a deeply positive perspective—one that has been shaped through both triumphs and trials.

GROWTH THROUGH STRUGGLE

It has come out of struggle and challenges, my near life ending car accident, cancer, and more. I know you have your challenges too. We all do.

"Strength and growth come only through continuous effort and struggle." —Napoleon Hill

I have learned through near death experiences, the promise and blessing of life. It has helped me keep a positive mindset and perspective.

You can too.

"It is during our darkest moments that we must focus to see the light." —Aristotle

There is light even in the darkness, you just have to look for it and focus on it.

Whatever you are going through, you will come out the other side, and then what are you going to do?

Remember *"Life Happens, and Then You Choose!"*

What are you choosing today?

The belief that you have no control over your life is a bunch of hogwash.

Remember, as my friend Nancy Barrows likes to say, *"you've made it through 100% of your worst days. "*

Don't let the negative thoughts and limiting beliefs take over your mind and your life. It can happen pretty quickly if you are not careful.

CHOOSE YOUR THOUGHTS

"You move in the direction of your strongest thoughts." —Craig Groeschel

And you get to choose those thoughts.

Why not start pre-deciding the outcomes you would like to happen. What would you like to see happen in your life?

It is the Reticular Activator in your brain that starts looking for what is consuming your mind.

A good example is when you get a new car. Suddenly, there are people all over town driving your car and there are cars the same color, everywhere. That is because your Reticular Activator is looking for exactly that.

In fact, do you know it is a scientific fact, that as you feed information to your brain through your thoughts, your brain actually rewires itself to start thinking that way.

It is amazing the control we actually have though our choices and thoughts. You can make a significant impact on your life though the way you think.

Remember, you get to choose your thoughts and as Craig Groeschel says, *"Change your thinking, change your life!"*

So move forward today, developing a positive perspective through all of your life journeys… good and bad.

I am definitely heading that direction. Ready for the next chapter in my journey, because I know…

God's Not Done With Me Yet!

6 - CHALLENGES PROVIDE OPPORTUNITY TO GROW

We all face challenges, but how we choose to see them makes all the difference. As I've shared in the past few chapters, I've had many opportunities to grow. It hasn't always been easy, but I believe it's been my choices—guided by faith—that have made the difference.

How about you?

CONVERSATION WITH A FRIEND

I recently had a conversation with a friend about the challenges of life. Like me, he's a verbal processor, and it was such a blessing to walk with him through his struggles, to listen, and to pray with him.

We are so much alike. I realized that he works through his challenges best when I simply let him talk. What he really needed from me was not answers, but presence—someone to listen, encourage, and give him space to process. He was already growing and learning from his situation, because he made the choice to reflect on both what he was doing right and what he needed to change.

Processing life is hard for all of us, but if we want to grow and become better versions of ourselves, we must be willing to look at our weaknesses and recognize that sometimes, we are part of the problem. There are always two sides to every situation, but we can always improve our side.

That kind of growth begins with perspective—how you choose to look at things. And when you let God guide your perspective, you'll always see more clearly.

It is truly your perspective that counts.

"Every challenge, every adversity, contains within it the seeds of opportunity and growth."
—Roy Bennett

It can be hard to see sometimes, but it is there. New opportunities lie just around the bend, and when you are looking for them, chances are you will find them.

So keep looking.

"There comes a point in your life when you realize your hardest times are your best times, too—you will see the rainbow of your life."
—Roy Bennett

LIFE TURNS

In 1993, before my car accident following my freshman year at Oregon State, I was feeling great about life. Despite some challenges, I had successfully completed my first year of college and enjoyed a wonderful year musically with the OSU Choir. I thought to myself, *"Nothing can stop me now…"*

And then it happened.

In an instant, my life was nearly gone—but through God's saving grace, I survived. God wasn't done with me yet.

The road back wasn't easy—I had to struggle and fight for it. After the accident, I was determined to return to Oregon State. The doctors almost laughed at the idea, telling me it wasn't possible. But deep inside, I knew I could do it. Determination kept me moving forward.

I created activities to keep me busy and active instead of sitting around. Because of my broken collarbones, I couldn't lift my arms above my head yet. So, I shot baskets on my home court underhanded. Look out, Rick Barry—here I come! I created a Wiffle ball golf course; it was a mini par 3. Isn't it ironic that the accident happened after golfing and driving away from a par 3 course?

These activities kept me moving, and I continued outpatient physical and occupational therapy. There were times I wanted to give up, but I just kept going.

I was truly becoming a better version of myself while overcoming these obstacles. And at this point, I didn't even understand that Jesus was with me every step of the way.

I was learning and growing.

After all, often our greatest growth and learning come through adversity.

It's true—through challenges we are refined and have the opportunity to learn and grow. It makes us better.

SILVER LINING

My mama used to say, *"There is always a silver lining."* In every situation, we can find the good. You just need to look for it. You just need to keep moving forward and maintain a positive attitude and perspective.

As you will see through this book, one of my favorite scriptures says, *"God works all things for the good of those who love him."* —Romans 8:28

That is so encouraging.

That keeps me moving!

"Obstacles don't have to stop you. If you run into a wall, don't turn around and give up. Figure out how to climb it, go through it, or work around it." —Michael Jordan

There is a way. We have to go through obstacles and challenges, but when we come out the other side, that is where amazing things happen.

Again, it boils down to your perspective. It is not a question of if challenges are going to come, because they will. It is what happens when they do that really makes the difference in your life.

"Life is not judged just by the heartbeats but by the way you accept and overcome the challenges of life." —Amit Ray

So be an overcomer. Look for ways to become better through the challenges and the bumps in your road.

Keep a positive perspective.

"Never sit back and wait for an opportunity to find you. Get up and search for one, and if it exists, find it!" —Victoria Addino

Step out and take a risk. Look for opportunities. Challenge yourself to be better today than you were yesterday.

BETTER TOGETHER

Come together with your community, because we are always better together.

"Don't be afraid of challenges. Let them take you somewhere new." —Sira Masetti

New challenges bring new opportunities. They lead to growth and strength. Don't shy away from the storms of life, because…

"There would be no rainbows without sunshine and rain." —Roy Bennett

The rain will come, but so will the opportunities. Remember, there is always sunshine somewhere.

Always keep in mind: **Life happens… and then you choose!**

It's up to you. Keep a healthy perspective today— and grow!

7 - OVERCOMING MORNING ANXIETY

(A portion of this taken from my book, "Befuddled? Live the Life You Choose!")

When I wake up, I often feel stressed and overwhelmed by everything I have to accomplish in the day ahead.

Is this you?

Many times, it starts with the information you were consuming the night before—books, social media, text messages, or even conversations with family and friends. That's why it's so important to be intentional about what you allow your mind to focus on before going to sleep.

"What you think about, you bring about."
—Bob Proctor

Your thoughts influence your mindset, shape your perspective, and impact not only what you do but also how you wake up in the morning.

YOUR MIND IS POWERFUL

So let me ask you: What are you allowing into your mind the moment you wake up? I talk about this in my book *Befuddled? Live the Life You Choose!*

The following is from chapter 1, "Fighting Through the Noise."

Each morning when I wake up, before I get out of bed, I tell myself three things.

First, that I am thankful for God, my beautiful wife, my family, my life, and the day to come.

Second, I tell myself I've got this. I know that with God's help I can conquer the day.

And third, I declare it's going to be an awesome day!

These are choices I make and communicate to myself every morning and this shapes my attitude and focus for the day ahead.

Give it a try...

1. Be thankful
2. You've got this
3. Today is going to be awesome!

BE THANKFUL

Beginning with the right mindset, gets your day off to a great start.

Next, I have my morning routine of good habits that include reading, prayer, and journaling. Also, I have a workout routine each morning. This gets me started on the right foot for the day.

It's important that we get started the right way, because there are so many things in life vying for our attention. All the noise around us calls out, saying, *"Look at me!"* Too often, without clear goals and direction, we become servants to whatever comes our way.

We need to take life one small step at a time. Just one small thing after the other. Small things soon become big things I love the quote. ***"One small positive thought in the morning can change your whole day."*** —Unknown

It's true, it can!

YOU'VE GOT THIS!

I go on to talk about how you can intentionally shape your mindset each day—and in doing so, shape the actions of your day.

Start by remembering to *think about what you think about.*

As Craig Groeschel says, **"Your life is always moving in the direction of your strongest thoughts."**

Be intentional about overcoming morning anxiety and fear by feeding your mind with positive input— through uplifting self-talk and life-giving sources. When you fill your mind with positive thoughts, you begin to push out the negative, anxious ones.

POSITIVE MINDSET

It is scientifically proven that a positive mindset can make you healthier and stronger. It relieves stress and reduces anxiety, both of which can negatively impact your body and mind.

Simply put—a positive mindset is good for you.

One of my oncologists at Oregon Health Sciences University(OHSU) once told me that the best thing I had going for me was my positive attitude. Well, after God's blessing and healing, of course.

I often think back to the many years my mom and dad instilled positive input into my life. They cared for me deeply and reminded me often that I was loved. They encouraged me to try new activities in school, supported me through the hard times, and celebrated the victories right alongside me. Through it all…

They taught me how to start my day right.

GOOD HABITS

I developed healthy habits early on—exercising regularly and focusing on what was important. As I grew into adulthood, I built on those habits and discovered what worked for me. Slowly, and with God's help, I developed the routines that guide my life today.

I believe it is crucial to start each day with both a plan and intentionality. Give yourself time and space to listen to the Lord, to speak positive truths over your life, and to silence the negative thoughts. In doing so, you set the tone for the rest of your day.

James Clear, author of **Atomic Habits**, teaches that the best way to build strong habits is to create triggers that lead to positive results. For example, he encourages people to set out their exercise clothes and shoes the night before as a cue for their morning workout. When I read this, I laughed and celebrated —because I was already doing it!

I thought to myself, ***"Yoo hoo! One small win for Russ!"***

No matter what your circumstances may be, you can restore a positive perspective by being intentional and building good habits each morning.
So today, what is your plan?

How are you going to restore—or continue—a positive mindset and perspective?
It's up to you!

Remember: **Life happens, and then you choose!**

8 - KEEP IT SIMPLE

This chapter brought to you by… Simplicity!

Everywhere you turn, life is pulling you in a thousand directions—emails, texts, social media, and now even AI demanding your attention. No wonder anxiety is on the rise! But what if the answer wasn't more noise, but less? What if the secret to joy was hidden in something ancient and timeless? One word: *Simplicity.*

KISS: Keep It Simple Strategically

Of course, this is a balancing act.

"Simplicity is an exact medium between too little and too much." —Sir Joshua Reynolds

Too often, we live at the extremes instead of finding harmony in a peaceful, balanced life. When we overcomplicate things, life quickly becomes difficult. But the truth is, simplicity is at the very foundation of life.

We were created to live by some beautifully simple principles:

- Love People & Give

- Live by the Golden Rule

- Be Thankful

- Connect & Build Community

How can these principles be helpful to you in your daily journey?

LOVE PEOPLE & GIVE

When you love others and focus on giving—not taking—life becomes so much easier. People are naturally drawn to you because you're not self-focused. And when you bring joy to others, you'll find joy comes right back to you—because positivity attracts positivity!

LIVE BY THE GOLDEN RULE

I'm a big Golden Rule guy. When you treat others the way you want to be treated, they will often reciprocate.

It creates harmony in life, and it only takes being kind, thoughtful, and empathetic to the situations of others.

BE THANKFUL

As I've already said, being thankful is the best way to start your day. It may not always be easy, but it is always worth the effort.

Thankfulness is a simple concept—and one we should take to heart each day.

CONNECT & BUILD COMMUNITY

We are truly better together.

When we connect and build community, we support each other through life's journey. And we all need that.

"Life is really simple, but we insist on making it complicated." —Confucius

Too often, we are our own worst enemy— overthinking, complicating, and stressing over even the simplest tasks. The solution? Slow down and simplify.

"It is not a daily increase, but a daily decrease. Hack away at the nonessentials." —Bruce Lee

Simplifying begins with removing the non-essentials. And a good place to start is by slowing down.

We are always in such a hurry. But as John Mark Comer reminds us, we need, *"The ruthless elimination of hurry!"*

DECLUTTER

Simplifying often requires hard choices and a willingness to declutter your current schedule.

When you declutter and simplify your life, you create space to process with intention and purpose. It takes effort—but you can do it.

In 2020, when COVID stopped the world, I was in the early planning stages of my current business. I felt strongly that God was leading me in this direction, but my sales and marketing management job was consuming 10–12 hours a day. By the time I got home, I only had enough energy left to spend with my beautiful wife.

When the world shut down, I suddenly had time on my hands. My wife said, *"If you believe God is moving you toward your own business, now is your chance."*

With that time and space to process, pray, and create, everything began to shift. Within five months, I had written and published a book, launched a podcast, spoken at online events, and started coaching several clients.

I chose to take what could have been a negative and, with intention, turn it into a positive.

So why not take a look at your own schedule? Give yourself the space to process life. Slow down and make time for God, your family, and yourself. A little self-care goes a long way.

ONE THING

It's a simple truth, but not always easy to practice: the KISS principle is something we must continually work at. Too often, we struggle because we complicate life instead of focusing on what really matters—our *One Thing*.

Gary Keller, the founder of Keller Williams Realty, asks a powerful question:

"What's the one thing I can do such that by doing it, everything else will become easier or unnecessary?"

At first, it may sound difficult—and at times, it can be. But when you choose to focus on your One Thing, the very thing most vital to your success, you'll find yourself living with less anxiety and more purpose in everything you do.

PRIORITIZE

Prioritize what is truly important.

For me, it's simple: **God, Family, Friends, and then Work.**

This prioritization helps me stay on track with my daily purpose and activities. It drives me toward significance in my life and relationships.

So today, remember to keep things simple. Live life with purpose—and on purpose.

Don't complicate life with so many details that you miss the simple truth.

"Our life is frittered away by detail. Simplify, simplify." —Henry David Thoreau

A simple principle, yes—but not an easy one. It takes focus, intention, and action.

So, roll up your sleeves, embrace the work, and start simplifying your life today.

9 - BEYOND THE FRUSTRATION

Do you ever get frustrated like me?

Sometimes it feels like life just isn't fair—and even worse, it can feel like God isn't listening!

"I've asked 'why' plenty of times. Now, I'm learning to ask 'where.' 'Where are You God? Give me eyes to see the thread of Your goodness running through." —Kaitlyn Bouchillon

Life is a journey—one we must walk through, step by step.

PET SCAN DILEMMA

One of my ongoing frustrations has been getting my quarterly PET scans during my cancer journey.

Because of the diabetes I developed through cancer treatment, I struggle with the preparation for these scans. The process requires fasting for six hours beforehand. That might sound simple, but for me it's complicated. When I fast, my blood sugar rises. I've been told the liver produces more glucose to sustain the body when fasting, but whatever the cause, my levels often climb above the limit required for the scan.

This creates a lot of stress the day before and the day of the scan. And these scans are critical—they're how my doctors monitor what's happening with the cancer in my body.

Through this challenge, I've had to learn to breathe deeply, release the stress, and trust God with the process. I've had to remind myself again and again: *He will make a way.*

If I'm honest, I wish it would all just go away. It wears on me, and it weighs on my whole family. But I've come to accept that this is part of the journey I must walk. I've had to learn new life rhythms—practices that help me navigate difficult times like this.

The same is true with my medications. Because of damage to some of my organs, I now have to take medicine to replace what they once did naturally. At first, it was discouraging. But I've learned not to fight it. Instead, I focus on what I *can* do rather than what I can't.

And this is where I come back to a simple but powerful truth:

Life happens... and then you choose.

LIFE CHALLENGES

Life's challenges are not magically taken away. They are meant to teach us, to strengthen us, and to help us grow.

God reminds us: **"I have told you these things, so that in me you may have peace. In this world you will have trouble. But take heart! I have overcome the world."** —John 16:33 (NIV)

As human beings, we naturally want life to always feel good, easy, and joyful. But the truth is, circumstances often beat us down and test our resolve. Even so, remember this: *you are not defined by your circumstances.*

God is always greater than our problems, and His power, love, and presence will carry you through every challenge you face.

MR. POSITIVE

I always want to be Mr. Positive and keep smiling. The problem is, even with a positive perspective, that isn't always possible. We all have down times— moments of struggle and frustration.

For people like me, that's hard. I often feel like I have to be positive all the time or I'm failing—but that simply isn't true.

"You don't have to be positive all the time. It's perfectly okay to feel sad, angry, annoyed, frustrated, scared, and anxious. Having feelings doesn't make you a 'negative person.' It makes you human." —Lori Deschene

That's right—it's called being human. It's called life, with its ups and downs, unexpected turns, and crazy moments we cannot explain. But through it all, we can still experience peace and strength.

TRUSTING IN GOD

I trust God for my peace.

"Then you will experience God's peace, which exceeds anything we can understand. His peace will guard your hearts and minds as you live in Christ Jesus." —Philippians 4:7

When I feel I cannot go on, I give it to Him. We all need to recognize that there is something greater than us—something beyond our control—that through faith brings us peace, hope, and love.

"Give your burdens to the Lord, and he will take care of you. He will not permit the godly to slip and fall." —Psalm 55:22

I try my best to give my frustrations to Him. It's my choice. What do you do with frustration? Where do you take it?

What is your choice?

"You've done it before and you can do it now. See the positive possibilities. Redirect the substantial energy of your frustration and turn it into positive, effective, unstoppable determination."
—Ralph Marston

I love that—*Unstoppable Determination!* That is what we need to keep going and consistently move in a positive direction… one step at a time. Keep your focus on the opportunities and outcomes, not the obstacle in front of you.

"To conquer frustration, one must remain intensely focused on the outcome, not the obstacles." —T.F. Hodge

ENVIRONMENT

Another important key is your environment. Who have you surrounded yourself with? Community matters.

"Surround yourself with people who empower you, believe in you, support you, uplift you, motivate you, appreciate you." —Unknown

The people that friend D. Scott Smith says… *"won't let you fail."*

When you do this, you're already moving in a positive direction with support all around you. As Jim Rohn said, *"You are the average of the five people you spend the most time with."*

Your environment is critical to your life. You will always be influenced by what surrounds you. The people and places around you will either add to your frustrations or help you through them. So make the choice today! Create a better environment with people who lift you up and walk beside you through life's challenges.

"A rising tide lifts all boats."
—President John F. Kennedy

When you surround yourself with people who are growing, positive, and encouraging, life becomes better. This is how you truly get *beyond the frustration.*

Remember, life is a journey—one we must walk through step by step, but never alone. With God leading the way, each step has purpose, every challenge brings growth, and every choice moves you closer to the life He created you to live.

Move beyond the frustration and make a significant impact today.

10 - SEEKING CLARITY & ALIGNMENT

There have been times in my life, like my college career at Oregon State University, that I felt lost and didn't know what I really needed. I didn't know where to turn.

I was out of alignment, and needed clarity.

If you are feeling weary, lacking clarity, and unsure of where to turn, you are not alone! The good news is… you don't have to have it all together to make an impact on life and on others. No matter who you are, you can make a difference in the lives of those around you simply by being yourself.

I love what Norman Vincent Peale says: *"One person can make a difference. You don't have to be a big shot. You don't have to have a lot of influence. You just have to have faith in your power to change things."*

Faith plays a tremendous role in this for me. I believe there is something so much bigger than us—a God who gives us strength, direction, hope, peace, and clarity. My faith is what sustains me on my life's journey, especially through the cancer journey I am walking now. I need God's strength. I need His direction. I need His hope, peace, and clarity.

And through Him, I find steadiness and alignment.

ALIGNMENT

We must be in alignment with God and with ourselves. Living with intention and purpose in everything we do is essential – that's what creates true alignment.

I love what Jeremiah 29:11 says: ***"For I know the plans I have for you," says the Lord. "They are plans for good and not for disaster, to give you a future and a hope."***

We can rest in the truth that we have purpose—and a God who gives us strength. Life is bigger than us, and we don't have to have it all together. We simply have to keep moving forward, one step at a time. When you intentionally seek clarity and purpose, alignment with God and with yourself becomes a reality. But let's be honest—it isn't always easy. Still, you *can* do it… one faithful step at a time.

BITS OF GOOD

"Do your little bit of good where you are; it is those little bits of good put together that overwhelm the world."
—Archbishop Desmond Tutu

You don't have to have all the answers. You don't need to see the entire journey ahead.

I've found myself in that position many times—uncertain about my next step and hoping God would send a lightning bolt with the answer right away. But life doesn't usually work like that. Life is a journey, and I had to learn to walk it one step at a time.

WHAT'S NEXT?

I entered my freshman year at Oregon State University thinking I had it all together. I had graduated high school in the top 10% of my class, been active in three sports, music, and drama, and life seemed to be going well. But suddenly, I was on my own—without my parents to guide me—and things started moving fast.

I thought to myself: ***What's next?***

The year began well socially—maybe a little too well —and good musically, as I was a music major. But my studies were another story—I was struggling. I still remember finals week, feeling completely lost in my mathematics and economics classes. Not knowing what else to do, I drove home with my best friend and roommate to spend time with my family decorating for Christmas, instead of studying.

The next day, I returned to school and promptly failed both classes. I hadn't developed good study habits, and left to my own system—or lack thereof—I was sinking. After earning a 1.79 GPA and being placed on academic probation, I once again asked myself: *What's next?*

The environment at Oregon State was very socially active, filled with partying, drinking, and other recreational activities I knew better than to get involved in—but I did anyway. I was off track and heading in the wrong direction, but everyone around me—through both their actions and words—made it seem perfectly normal. *This is just what college kids do.*

Looking back, this was a step in my journey where I had a lot of maturing and growing to do. At the time, it felt unsettling, but it forced me to figure things out. As tough as it was, the experience made me stronger and better in the long run. The truth is, the greatest growth in our lives often comes through adversity. It may not be enjoyable, but adversity sharpens our focus and pushes us to find a way forward.

FOCUS

Clarity and alignment come when we learn to focus on how to move through difficult circumstances. This is a reality we all face at some point in our lives.

That's where faith comes in—faith in the power God has given us to change things. We have a choice every minute of every day.

Life happens, and then you choose!

You get to choose whether to focus, get aligned, and gain clarity through your journey. You get to choose to redirect your life onto a path that will take you where you want to go.

So... enjoy your journey, one step at a time.
As Martin Luther King Jr. said: ***"You don't have to see the whole staircase, just take the first step."***

So take the first step. Start your journey.

Life is your greatest teacher, and the journey you are on is a blessing—if you keep a good perspective and commit to learning and growing with each step. Soon, more steps will appear in front of you. As you keep moving forward, things will begin to clear, and you will gain wisdom and strength along the way.

The journey before us brings both struggles and celebrations. But the key is this:

Keep moving.

When you keep moving forward, you will not only become stronger—you will also inspire and impact the people around you. And as you walk step by step with God, you will discover clarity, alignment, and purpose that will transform your life. So keep moving, keep believing, and keep choosing life—because the world needs the very best of you.

11- LEARNING THROUGH LIFE CHANGES

Life is always moving and changing. The journey is full of ups and downs.

This past month, I lost a dear friend, and at the same time, my house seemed to be falling apart.

My friend had battled breast cancer years ago and had been cancer-free for over 20 years. She had been one of my biggest encouragers throughout my own cancer journey. After returning from a vacation, she wasn't feeling well. The doctors told her the cancer had reappeared—in her bones and lungs. Within just two months, she was gone.

It was a hard, painful loss.

And during that same season, life kept throwing curveballs. Our air conditioning broke down, and we had to find a way to replace it without the resources to make it happen. Then our refrigerator stopped cooling, the toilet in our master bath broke, and finally, the washing machine gave up.

By the grace of God, we were able to take care of the appliances, and I managed to fix the toilet. But it wasn't easy. And through it all, the loss of my friend weighed heavily on me.

Still, with God's help and a fresh perspective, I made it through. Along the way, I learned lessons, and God showed me things I needed to see.

"The journey may be messy, but with faith, every step has purpose." —Unknown

It's true. Even in the middle of the mess, you are learning and growing. Sometimes it's just hard to see through all the challenges.

So where do you start? Begin your navigation with a positive attitude and perspective.

Because with God's strength, and the right mindset, even the messiest seasons can become a testimony of faith, hope, and perseverance.

ATTITUDE

At the beginning of my cancer journey, my oncologist told me something I'll never forget: ***"Your positive attitude will be the number one thing that helps you fight this disease and recover."***

That truth goes far beyond cancer—it applies to every part of life. We often don't realize how much the way we think impacts our health, our relationships, and the direction of our journey.

A positive perspective changes everything. And part of that perspective is realizing we need help along the way.

The Bible reminds us in Psalm 118:14, ***"The LORD is my strength and my song; he has given me victory."***

God gives us strength. The community gives us support. And Jesus meets us right in the middle of the mess! I believe He is faithful, and He will guide us through any tough circumstance.

Never forget—community matters. The people around you can help you navigate through life's challenges, reminding you that you are never alone in the journey.

THE JOURNEY

Life is full of twists, turns, and surprises. Often the unexpected leaves you feeling lost or overwhelmed. But here's the truth: you don't have to face it alone. God is with you, and every step of your journey matters.

"God's plans for you are always greater than the challenges you face." —Unknown

As we travel, we grow stronger and gain wisdom—if we are present and paying attention along the way.

To move forward, you have to take risks—step out in faith and trust that you're walking the path God designed for you. As you navigate life, the lessons you learn and the experiences you gain don't just shape you—they can bless others. When your journey helps someone else through their challenges, you strengthen them... and yourself. That's when life becomes significant. That's when the journey truly matters.

"Strength grows in the moments when you think you can't go on but keep going anyway."
—Unknown

That strength to persevere is what makes life's moments significant and makes a true impact on others.

Maintaining your faith fills you with hope and keeps you moving forward.

"Faith doesn't make things easy, it makes them possible." —Luke 1:37

LEARNING

Life can get messy. Plans fall apart. Circumstances don't go your way. But here's the good news: every challenge carries a lesson. Every setback holds an opportunity to grow into the person God created you to be.

"Growth and meaning often come dressed as chaos." —Unknown

It is an imperfect picture of God's perfect plan for your life.

"Life's beauty is in its imperfections; embrace them and keep moving forward." —Unknown

Perspective is everything. How you see your journey shapes how you experience it.

And there it is… embrace what is and move forward in spite of the circumstances.

I made a choice with the loss of my friend to look at what God did through my life in that experience. He allowed me the blessing of seeing her and praying with her at the end. I also discovered how God had used my cancer journey to encourage her all the way to her finish line. Today, I am comforted knowing she is safe with the Lord and free from pain.

Through my house challenges, I also learned patience and a deeper dependence on God. More than once, He worked miracles that allowed us to take care of what was needed.

Life happened—and I chose to trust God and move forward in spite of the circumstances.

You can overcome the mess of life by choosing a healthy perspective and a strong mindset.

This messy life is worth the fight—and it doesn't define you! Hold on to hope, stay strong, and keep pressing forward. With God by your side, the best is always yet to come.

So get out there and live your best life now!

"Be strong and courageous! Do not be afraid or discouraged. For the LORD your God is with you wherever you go." —Joshua 1:9

12 - IMPACT YOUR WORLD

Through my cancer journey, I have been led by God to be a positive light and an encouragement to others in the midst of everything I've faced. I have always wanted to impact others for good, and I believed that —with God's help—I could turn my situation into inspiration for others.

How?

By choosing to live out my faith in spite of the challenges before me. I believe that keeping a good perspective, even through trials, encourages others in whatever they are going through… because we all have "stuff."

So once again… **Life Happens, and Then You Choose!**

I love the book *"Choose Joy"* by Chip Ingram. In it, he introduces what he calls the **divine equation:**

C + P = E

Circumstances + Perspective = Experience

Chip explains it this way:

"Living above your circumstances occurs when your perspective interprets your circumstances, rather than your circumstances determining your perspective."

I believe this is absolutely true. Early on in my journey, I made the decision to listen to God's leading and to choose a good perspective, no matter what I was facing.

And trust me—there have been moments when my situation left me feeling completely worn out. I have been exhausted, sick, and ready to give up.

People often ask me if I'm happy all the time, because I tend to have a very upbeat, outgoing personality. My answer is simple: **No, I'm not always happy.** There are times when I am very far from happy. But even in those moments, I hold onto perspective. I remind myself that—with God's help— better days are ahead. I have hope.

Through it all, I've learned there are four areas that truly impact my world. They are simple, yet life-changing: **Passion, Purpose, Perspective, and People.**

These four areas can transform your life, give you clarity, and position you to live with real impact.

THE FOUR P's

How can you truly make a difference in this life? By living out the **Four P's**, you can impact your own life, touch the lives of others, and become a true world-changer.

Passion

Let's start with **Passion.**

"If you feel like there's something out there that you're supposed to be doing, if you have a passion for it, then stop wishing and just do it."
—Wanda Sykes

I truly believe passion is the fuel that drives both your life and your purpose.

"Nothing great in the world has ever been accomplished without passion."
—Georg Wilhelm Friedrich Hegel

When you are passionate about something, you gain a new level of drive and focus. Passion gives you the energy to keep moving forward and the determination to accomplish great things.

And here's the best part—passion naturally leads you to the next "P."

Purpose

Next is **Purpose.**

We were all created by God for a specific purpose. So, the question is: *What is yours?* Why are you here?

I love this thought from T.D. Jakes: *"If you can't figure out your purpose, figure out your passion. For your passion will lead you right into your purpose."*

Your passion is a clue that points directly to your purpose. And once you step into that purpose, it brings freedom, fulfillment, and joy—because you're exactly where you were designed to be.

Purpose aligns with your God-given talents and abilities. When you are walking in it, life feels like it *flows*. You're on top of your game, and more importantly, you're in the center of God's plan for your life.

And that alignment brings something we all desire: true happiness.

"True happiness… is not attained through self-gratification, but through fidelity to a worthy purpose." —Helen Keller

Living with purpose gives you joy, strength, and direction as you pursue what God intended for you to accomplish.

Perspective

The third "P" is **Perspective.**

As I have said previously, Perspective shapes the way you see life—and it drives your actions.

How are you truly looking at your life right now? Remember, you don't always get to choose your circumstances, but you always get to choose your response.

"The only thing you sometimes have control over is perspective. You don't have control over your situation. But you have a choice about how you view it." —Chris Pine

Life happens. But then—you choose how to see it.

"Life happens for you, not to you." —Ed Mylett

Your perspective determines whether you see obstacles or opportunities, setbacks or setups, problems or possibilities. And that choice will shape the direction of your life.

People

The final "P" is **People.**

After God and His love, connection to others and community is the foundation of life. We were never meant to do life alone.

You can change the world when you walk alongside others.

"There is no power for change greater than a community discovering what it cares about."
— Margaret J. Wheatley

We are truly better together—especially when you surround yourself with people who care deeply, encourage you, and intentionally walk with you to make life better.

You become your community.

Remember the wisdom of Jim Rohn: *"You are the average of the five people you spend the most time with."*

So, choose wisely. Spend your time with people who are driven, faith-filled, and living their God-given purpose—people who lift others while they climb.

LIVING THE FOUR P's

Passion. Purpose. Perspective. People.

These are my **Four P's of Life.** When you live them out, you won't just change your own world—you'll make a lasting impact on the world around you.

13 - CHANGE YOUR THINKING, CHANGE YOUR LIFE

What did you think about when you woke up this morning?

I made the intentional choice to start with positive, grateful, and encouraging thoughts. That's how I launched my day in the right direction.

But it wasn't always that way. Sure, I'm an upbeat, positive guy overall—but there was a time when I let my morning thoughts control me and hold me back. I would hear that inner voice say things like:

"You're tired. You don't want to get up. Nothing good is going to happen this morning, so you won't miss anything. No one cares if you show up at work anyway."

Have you ever had a similar experience?

Negative thoughts like that can drag us down quickly. They set us on the wrong path from the very beginning. They slow us down, and worse, they stop us from stepping into the good things God has already prepared for us.

"Our lives are always moving in the direction of our strongest thoughts. What we think shapes who we are." —Craig Groeschel

Our thoughts literally control our lives. When we keep a positive attitude, we are far more likely to act in positive ways. The opposite is also true—and that is not a great option. I always say, *"Think Positive and Get Your Hopes Up!"* When you believe in yourself, and when you believe life is going to be awesome, you will move in that direction.

LIFE DIRECTION

"Your life is a reflection of your thoughts. If you change your thinking, you change your life."
—Brian Tracy

Don't believe the lies you are told. Don't allow people or circumstances to define who you are.

You must drive the narrative. Write your own story! Think back to when you were young. Did you ever have a so-called friend tell you something about yourself that wasn't true? Maybe you believed it, simply because they were your friend. Even though it wasn't true, it still hurt—and it made you wonder if that's what others thought about you.

That's why you can't just accept someone else's narrative. Just because a statement is made with confidence doesn't make it true. Don't let lies, assumptions, or the opinions of others shake your confidence or damage your self-image. Stand firm. Don't give others the power to control who you are.

SELF-TALK

I am a huge believer in positive self-talk. The way you talk to yourself drives the direction of your life. Tell yourself the truth: *You are a good person. You are a person of value. You have amazing things to offer this world.* Yes, there will always be negative voices—both in your head and from the world around you, but you get to choose which voice you will listen to. The best way to silence the destructive voices is to drown them out with positive, faith-filled self-talk.

FEAR

Negative voices always drive fear. But God never intended for fear to control your life. You can accomplish great things! You just need to believe it, declare it, and step forward in faith.

"God has not given us a spirit of fear, but of power and of love and of a sound mind."
—2 Timothy 1:7

That's right—you have a sound mind! A God-given mind designed to accomplish amazing things. Every day, you get to choose who drives the narrative in your life. Don't hand over that power to others. Go on the offense. Take the initiative. Live as the person God has called you to be. And let me say it one more time, because this truth is crucial:

"A lie believed as truth will affect your life as if it were true." —Craig Groeschel

So—don't believe the lies!

BASKETBALL

I always loved basketball, and I was a good player. I began my high school career starting as a guard on the sophomore team. I was one of the top scorers and even got the chance to play a few games with the JV team, one level higher. Basketball was always my favorite sport, even though I played three sports every year.

During the football season of my sophomore year, I was quarterback of the JV team. The JV coach also happened to be the varsity basketball coach—and we did not get along. Honestly, if it hadn't been for the support of the other coaches, he could have ruined my high school football career.

When basketball season came around, I had a great coach for the sophomore team, and I really enjoyed that year. But I also knew that the following season I would have to play for the varsity coach—and I had a problem with that. I let fear creep in. I started to believe the lies I told myself: *"He won't play me… I'll have a horrible season… it's not worth it."* So, I didn't even go out for basketball my junior year.

Looking back now, I realize I let one person, fear, and lies derail my high school basketball career. I had value to bring to the team, but I talked myself out of it. And all for reasons that weren't even true.
Can you relate to this story?

Have you been derailed in the middle of a good career you enjoyed?

YOU HAVE VALUE

You are valuable. You are unique. You have been gifted with talents and abilities designed for impact.

"So if both the Bible and modern science teach us that our lives are moving in the direction of our strongest thoughts, then we need to ask ourselves: Do I like the direction my thoughts are taking me?" —Craig Groeschel

Where are your thoughts taking you?

CHANGE

Do you need to make a change?

"Change your thinking. Change your life! Your thoughts create your reality. Practice positive thinking. Act the way you want to be, and soon you will be the way you act." —Les Brown

It takes practice to think positively—but you can do it! No matter what you are going through, you can change your thinking. Remember: *"Life Happens… and Then You Choose!"* So choose positive thinking.

"You cannot control what happens to you, but you can control how you frame it."
—Craig Groeschel

Frame your life in a way that blesses others and builds you up. Feed yourself truth, not lies. Choose positive thinking, choose positive action—and watch your life change. It's up to you! You get to live a life that shines God's light and inspires others!"

Live a life full of joy, hope, and impact!

14 - THE GRATITUDE PERSPECTIVE

What is your perspective on life? Does it start with gratitude?

"Being grateful all the time isn't easy. But it's when you least feel thankful that you are most in need of what gratitude can give you: Perspective. Gratitude can transform any situation. It alters your vibration, moving you from negative energy to positive." —Oprah Winfrey

When you wake up, one small grateful thought can change and redirect your entire day. God can use it to build positive momentum and get you moving in the right direction—or you can choose the alternative, which can completely derail you.

The choice is up to you. You need that positive energy to launch your day in the right direction from the very beginning.

MORNING ROUTINE

This is why I'm such a big believer in a good morning routine. How you start your day sets the tone for everything that follows. We all have some kind of morning routine, even if it looks like flying out of bed, jumping into the shower, throwing on whatever is halfway clean, and dashing out the door. That's a recipe for stress, imbalance, and frustration.

A better approach is to be intentional. Give yourself time to breathe, pray, think, and prepare. Let your mind wake up and focus on what's ahead. When you start on solid ground, the day becomes easier to handle. When you start in chaos, you're behind the eight ball from the very beginning.

ACTIVE GRATITUDE

Gratitude isn't just something you say—it's something you live.

"As we express our gratitude, we must never forget that the highest form of appreciation is not to utter words, but to live by them."
—John F. Kennedy

It starts with attitude, and then it flows into action. Gratitude is a choice only you can make.

"Always have an attitude of gratitude."
—Sterling K. Brown

When you live with thankfulness and abundance, good things happen.

YOUR BEST LIFE

If you want to be happy and live your best life now, be grateful!

"I am happy because I'm grateful. I choose to be grateful. That gratitude allows me to be happy."
—Will Arnett

Happiness flows from gratitude. It's an intentional choice we need to make day after day. When you focus on your blessings, you fuel the pursuit of your dreams and goals. Gratitude is a mindset that works in life, relationships, and business.

I choose each day to be grateful through every situation of my life—even in my battle with cancer and the physical challenges that remain from treatment.

I know… you may be saying, *"No way!"* But it's true.

Notice I said *through every situation.* I am definitely not grateful for every situation.

With God's help, I look for the good that can come from even the hardest circumstances. If I embrace what is happening and choose to keep the right perspective, I will learn and grow through every moment.

I know there are better things ahead, so I will be grateful not only for what I've already experienced, but also for what is yet to come.

"Be grateful for what you already have while you pursue your goals. If you aren't grateful for what you already have, what makes you think you would be happy with more?" —Roy T. Bennett

That's a powerful question! Look at all the blessings you already have. Practice being grateful daily.

CULTIVATE GRATITUDE

Gratitude doesn't just happen—you have to cultivate it. It's a habit, a discipline, and a mindset of success.

"Cultivate the habit of being grateful for every good thing that comes to you, and to give thanks continuously. And because all things have contributed to your advancement, you should include all things in your gratitude."
—Ralph Waldo Emerson

If you aren't already, start being thankful for all you have. Make it a daily habit. Choose gratitude at every opportunity. Show gratitude to God, to the people who bless your life, and to the circumstances that grow you.

Gratitude brings joy, strengthens relationships, and draws people together.

"No matter what happens in life, be good to people. Being good to people is a wonderful legacy to leave behind." —Taylor Swift

BEING GOOD STARTS WITH GRATITUDE

If you want to start things right, start with gratitude. How you begin each day determines the steps you'll take and the actions that will propel you forward.

How you start and how you treat others will determine your legacy. How do you want to be remembered?

Living with a gratitude perspective will shape how others see you, how you impact the world, and the legacy you leave.

Choose to be mindful of others. The gratitude perspective is about thinking beyond yourself—leading with kindness, compassion, and love. This is how God wants you to live. This is the roadmap to joy, fulfillment, and the satisfaction of a life well lived.

So let me ask: how do you want to leave things when you're gone? Do you want to make an impact that lasts long after your time on earth is over? If so, you must be intentional now.

Make good decisions. Treat people with respect. Live with gratitude. Step up today for the impact you want to make tomorrow.

You've got this!

15 - ROUTINES CREATE SUCCESS

"The secret of your future is hidden in your daily routine." —Mike Murdock

It's true! Your habits and routines are what drive your daily productivity and ultimately determine your success—or lack of it.

MY ROUTINES

I'm definitely someone who has to create routines for my own good. I'm a right-brained, creative type who would fly by the seat of my pants if I could. But life doesn't work well that way—especially when you become a husband and a father.

I had to learn to be responsible for myself, my beautiful wife, and our kids. Without routines and good habits, I would have lost most everything I owned and would never have been on schedule.

My mama used to joke that I'd lose my head if it wasn't attached—and she wasn't wrong!

Over time, I've learned the value of routines in almost every area of life. Someone once told me they thought I was a Type A personality, and I laughed. I am not naturally detailed or organized—unless I *choose* to be.

When I was young, my room was a disaster. I could never find my stuff, and I paid little attention to details or what was happening around me. My beautiful wife might argue that some of that hasn't changed, but I've definitely improved by being intentional with my routines!

Life has a way of teaching lessons. For example, shortly after I got my driver's license, I set a 16 oz glass bottle of Coke on top of my car while trying to juggle too many things at once. Then I drove off— leaving a mess of glass and soda all over the driveway that I had to clean up.

I learned a simple lesson and routine that day: *always* put my drink inside the car first, then handle the rest before I start driving. One small habit spared me from repeating the same mistake.

Routines and good habits protect us from unnecessary messes—literally and figuratively.

CHANGE

Sometimes, success requires a change in your routines.

"You will never change your life until you change something you do daily. The secret of your success is found in your daily routine."
—John C. Maxwell

Routines are simply daily habits that guide your life. Some are great, and some aren't so great. The good news is—you get to choose.

When I decided to start running in the mornings with my dog, I built a new routine/habit of laying out my jogging shoes and the leash the night before. It was a visual reminder to follow through. Later, I discovered this principle in James Clear's book *Atomic Habits*: *make it obvious.*

"Habits are the compound interest of self-improvement." —James Clear

Even a 1% improvement each day compounds into major growth over time.

If you want better results, start by developing intentional, positive habits that lead you to your God-given goals.

DAILY ROUTINE

"A daily routine built on good habits and disciplines separates the most successful among us from everyone else. The routine is exceptionally powerful." —Darren Hardy

I learned that once I made the change, I had to stay consistent. That routine helped me get into better shape and better health.

The truth is, I had to stop sleeping in and being lazy with my mornings. There are many ways to start the day—but "late and without coffee" is not one of them!

Let's be honest—we all wake up a little out of balance. Most mornings, the temptation is to hit snooze, dread the day, or worry about everything ahead. But that doesn't set you up for success.

INTENTIONAL CHOICE

That was me—until I made an intentional choice to change. I started getting up earlier to give myself space and time.

Did it suddenly become easy? No. I didn't leap out of bed singing every morning. Sometimes it was hard to get moving—but I did it anyway, because I chose to.

I truly believe you can *"Live the Life You Choose!"* In fact, the title of my book ***Befuddled? Live the Life You Choose*** came out of one of those messy mornings where I had to push myself forward, even while feeling out of sync.

A morning routine is vital. It requires intentional choice and a positive mindset.

MY MORNING SELF-TALK ROUTINE

As I mentioned before, before I even get out of bed, I remind myself of three things:

1. **I AM THANKFUL**. Thankful for God, my beautiful wife, my family, and my friends.

2. **I'VE GOT THIS**. God has blessed me with gifts, talents, and abilities to do what needs to be done.

3. **TODAY IS GOING TO BE AWESOME!** Life is filtered through the lens we choose. I choose my "Awesome Filter," so when challenges come—and they do—they don't seem so bad.

When we start our day with gratitude, confidence, and a positive perspective, life is lighter, more productive, and far more joyful.

BE INTENTIONAL AND CONSISTENT

If you want to succeed, you must be intentional about your habits and consistent in your routines.

"With consistency and reps and routine, you're going to achieve your goals and get where you want to be." —Mandy Rose

Doing the right thing once won't take you far. Doing it faithfully builds momentum that carries you to greatness.

Focus on what matters most—Body, Mind, and Spirit. Great athletes like Patrick Mahomes thrive not just because of talent, but because of holistic routines that sharpen all three.

Mahomes once said: *"I try to just focus on the same routine every single day."* That consistency has made him a champion.

LIVE YOU BEST LIFE NOW

So today—make the choice. Pay attention to what's important. Build routines that bring you closer to your goals.

As David Wolfe said, *"My daily routine is to make every day the best day."*

Why choose to live *your best life now—every day*?

It's up to you—so be intentional, be consistent, and build routines that lead to the success God has in store for you!

16 - FOCUS: THE DRIVER OF YOUR DESTINY

I am not a super-detailed or highly focused individual. Honestly, my beautiful wife is the detail-oriented one, and I am the right-brained, creative one. I'm the encourager, driver, the idea guy.

When we first got married, I quickly realized this. I let her take control of the finances, and she also handled the planning for our honeymoon, a place to live, and our first furniture. She worked through the details, and I took care of the action.

Just to show you why I shouldn't be the one in charge of the details—after a few years of marriage, she asked me to take over the finances. Let's just say… I messed them up. In fact, after years of me handling them, we had to work together to get things back on track.

It's not that I can't do it—it's that I don't always focus well or pay close attention to detail.

What I am, though, is decisive. I'm a "make it happen" kind of guy. Action is my middle name. I'm a driver. And once I matured and learned the importance of focus, I began to align myself with the goals I wanted to accomplish—and the details needed to get there.

Here's the best part: once I finally understood how vital those details are, I also learned to hire the right people to handle them so I could focus on my strengths. I truly believe God designed us this way on purpose. He gives each of us unique gifts and talents, while also reminding us that we're not meant to do life alone.

"Now you are the body of Christ, and each one of you is a part of it." —1 Corinthians 12:27

Let's look at the word **"focus."**

According to *Merriam-Webster*, **"focus"** has several definitions. The most common are concentration and a central point. It can mean concentrating attention or effort, adjusting an eye or camera lens, or being the center of interest.

Noun:
Focus is defined as a central point of attraction, attention, or activity. It can also describe a point where rays of light converge or diverge.

Verb:
Focus means to concentrate attention or effort, or to adjust an eye or camera to a particular range. It can also mean to come to a focus or converge.

It is very important to have focus in your life. And that focus should be on what is most important—what will help you make an impact on life.

Do you have trouble maintaining your focus?

Are you unsure what to focus on?

"Your life is controlled by what you focus on."
—Tony Robbins

So be intentional about who you let into your life and what you choose to focus on.

INTENTIONAL THOUGHT

You are always moving toward the things you think about the most. Your thoughts direct your actions, which is why your focus is so important. It must be intentional and well thought out.

If you are unfocused and living life haphazardly, you won't end up where you want to go. You'll end up somewhere—but it won't be by choice.

"Nothing that happens in life, happens by accident." —Unknown

Where do you want to go?

Are you struggling to find the way?

FOCUSED SOLUTIONS

"Focus on the solution, not on the problem." —Jim Rohn

Too many people get caught up focusing on their problems and letting fear and anxiety direct their path. Fear is a great distractor—it always leads us somewhere we don't want to go.

Are you intentionally seeking solutions, or are you distracted and fumbling through life without direction?

There is so much noise around us—comparison, doubt, and the opinions of others—that creates anxiety and feeds our limiting beliefs.

"Ignore the noise, focus on your work."
—Unknown

In my book, ***Befuddled? Live the Life You Choose!*** I talk about fighting through the noise. When you intentionally ignore it and focus on what matters, you find clarity, productivity, and success.

GROWTH

"What you focus on grows." —Esther Hicks

Whatever you give your attention to multiplies. Focus on the good, and you'll find more good in your life. Focus on the negative, and worry will consume you.

"Always remember, your focus determines your reality." —George Lucas

Your reality is shaped by your thoughts and focus because your thoughts drive your actions.

If you constantly tell yourself why you *can't* do something, you won't get much done. But if you choose to believe you *can* and keep your focus on positive results, you'll be amazed at what you accomplish.

MAKE IT HAPPEN

"Don't make excuses for why you can't get it done. Focus on all the reasons why you must make it happen." —Ralph Marston

What outcomes are you truly aiming for?
Success doesn't happen by chance—it happens when you are determined, focused, and intentional.

The truth is simple: Focus = Outcome.

So why not choose to focus on the positive instead of the negative? Focus on what you *can* do, not what you can't. Pour your energy into what is possible. Keep moving forward with determination and a can-do attitude.

"Focus on your strengths, not your weaknesses."
—Gary Vaynerchuk

At the end of the day, it all comes down to one simple truth:

It's up to you.

It's your choice.

Each moment brings new opportunities to move closer to what you're truly after. Take ownership— because no one else can live your life for you.

Obstacles and distractions will come. Doubt will whisper in your ear and try to derail you. But when you intentionally choose to focus on what matters most, great things happen.

Take small steps forward with purpose. Build unstoppable momentum. The key isn't perfection— it's progress.

Through my 61 years, I've learned to keep taking baby steps forward, even when life gets tough. And if I can do it, so can you. It's okay if you don't have it all figured out. Just don't stop—that's when you get stuck.

You were created with a purpose. If you dig deep and choose to keep your focus on what you can do, you are capable of more than you realize.

Stay focused on the purpose God created you to live. Keep your eyes on Him and you will find the strength, courage, and clarity to keep moving forward. With His help, you can finish strong and live the life you were created to live!

17 - A LIGHT OF HOPE

Have you ever stopped to wonder why you're here?

In my fourth year at Oregon State University, I was seriously questioning my purpose and direction. I felt off track, uncertain, and honestly—lost.

I was searching for hope and meaning in all the wrong places. I wasn't sure if I would ever graduate, get married, or live the kind of life I had always dreamed about.

Then, by God's divine intervention, everything began to change.

I met with my counselor, who created a plan for me: finish two more terms, complete an internship in the spring, and I would graduate with a Bachelor of Science in Communications.

Not long after, I met my now beautiful wife, who gave me all the encouragement and incentive I needed to stay the course. Around that same time, I found the

Lord—and with my newfound faith, I began to structure my life for success.

Suddenly, I had faith, purpose, and passion to make a difference in my world.

There was a light of hope.

"The two most important days in your life are the day you are born and the day you find out why."
—Mark Twain

CREATED WITH PURPOSE

You weren't created by accident. Your life holds meaning, purpose, and divine intention.

You were created to be a beacon of hope—a light on a hill—guiding others through the storms of life.

And here's the truth: every day is a choice.

You can choose to shine.

You can choose to lift others up.

You can choose to offer hope in the struggle and remind someone that they have value.

"Let your light shine for all to see, for the glory of the Lord rises to shine on you."
—Isaiah 60:1, (NCV)

This isn't just encouragement—it's a calling.

I believe we were all made to reflect the light of God into a dark world, and your light matters more than you know.

HELPING OTHERS

"Be the light that helps others see." —Unknown

So many around you need the light inside of you. You can make a real difference in someone's world today. Even if it's only one person, that's an incredible gift and power given to you by God!

"There is always light. If only we're brave enough to see it. If only we're brave enough to be it."
— Amanda Gorman

Are you brave enough to step out today and be that light? Sometimes it takes vulnerability—sharing what you are going through. That honesty encourages others to believe they too can overcome their struggles.

Remember, *Life Happens... and Then You Choose!*

I've been blessed this past three years to share my cancer journey, inspiring and encouraging others by showing how God continues to sustain me through it all. He gave me hope and allowed His light to shine through me.

What an honor and a blessing! Even in the roughest times, I know God is with me, and that I have His Light and His Hope.

LIGHT THE CANDLE

"There are two ways of spreading light: to be the candle or the mirror that reflects it."
—Edith Wharton

You can be the candle that shines in the darkness, giving hope to others, and you can also be the mirror that reflects what God is doing—in your life and in the lives of those around you. Both are gifts from God. Be the reflection you want to see.

Let me encourage you today: be filled with hope. Not a shallow hope that fades when life gets hard, but a deep, unshakable hope that comes from knowing who you are and whose you are.

We all face struggles. Life can feel heavy, uncertain, even overwhelming. But in the midst of the storm, you have a choice. You can choose to hold on to the light that comes from God—His love, His promises, His purpose.

And when you do, something beautiful happens: you shine.

You become a light for others. You become a voice of encouragement, a source of strength, and a reminder that God is still working—even when life feels messy.

You don't have to have it all figured out. God already does, and His plan is in motion.

All you need is faith and a willing heart. When you carry God's hope inside you, it overflows into others. His light through you becomes life-giving.

So take heart—you were made for this.

Let your light shine boldly—not in your own strength, but in His.

"As we work to create light for others, we naturally light our own way."
—Mary Anne Radmacher

ENCOURAGE

When you spread the light, you illuminate not only the path of others—but your own.

With God's help, you can be the one who lifts others up, offers encouragement, and, in the process, discovers renewed strength and hope for yourself. It's the boomerang effect—what you give always finds its way back to you.

Kindness. Compassion. Joy. Hope.

Your actions become seeds of blessing for others, and in time, those seeds find their way back into your own life.

You don't need a spotlight to shine. You make a difference with one simple step forward each day. You may feel like only one light, but your light can spark thousands.

"Just as one candle lights another and can light thousands of other candles, so one heart illuminates another heart and can illuminate thousands of other hearts." —Leo Tolstoy

You have the power to influence your world—starting today. So why not spread that light? Why not be a difference-maker and a world-changer?

The choice is yours. Don't let life's challenges dim your light.

Keep moving forward. Stay grounded in God's truth. Be the light.

Because when you do, you'll discover something powerful: You really do get to live the life you choose.

18 - THE LONG AND WINDING ROAD

Life can be a long and winding road. It's full of ups and downs, twists and turns—but here's the key: no matter what comes your way, you must keep moving forward.

"Good things are coming down the road. Just don't stop walking." —Robert Warren Painter Jr.

I've had my share of twists and turns, and I know you have too. But every challenge, every setback, and every detour has the potential to shape you into something stronger. One of the greatest examples in my life of this truth comes from sports—always moving, always changing, always demanding more than I thought I had to give. And in the process, teaching me that victory only comes when you refuse to quit.

FOOTBALL

I remember playing football in high school and going through conditioning. We had to run 240-yard sprints in full gear. There were moments I just wanted to stop, but I knew the game was coming on Friday night. There were rewards ahead for the pain and exhaustion I was enduring. I was becoming stronger and better because of it.

I chose to keep putting one foot in front of the other, pushing beyond what I thought I could do. And guess what? I did it. I accomplished my goal and made it to the game—the reward.

So here's my advice to you: keep moving forward. Even when it's hard. Even when you can't see what lies ahead. Remember, the pain you're enduring now will make you stronger for what's to come.

SINGLE STEP

Remember, *"A journey of 1,000 miles begins with a single step."* —Lao Tzu

And every step counts.

Life is a journey in everything you do—including your business.

When I was in elementary school, we moved to a property with five acres of forest. Our neighbors also had acres of trees, so we were always exploring. Sometimes, when I was out there alone, I would get lost. I'd stop, take a breath, look around, and get my bearings. Then I'd take one step… then another… and before long, I was back in familiar territory.

The same is true in life—one step at a time leads you back to where you need to be.

FEAR

Don't let fear stop you from taking that next step. Challenges will come, but keep moving forward. What you're looking for may be just around the corner.

If you stop now, you may never know what you could have accomplished or where you could have gone.

Keep going. One step at a time.

"Fear kills more dreams than failure ever will."
—Suzy Kassem

Don't let fear kill your dreams.

Life can be difficult, but with purpose and intention, you will find your way.

DIFFICULT ROADS

Zig Ziglar once said, *"Difficult roads often lead to beautiful destinations. The best is yet to come."*

With that perspective, how can you fail?

Yes, there will be bumps and potholes in the road, but as you learn to navigate them, life's possibilities begin to turn into your realities.

I remember when I first began my music journey back in fourth grade. I picked up the trumpet and started to play, and before long, I was singing at special events with my classmates. Even though I came from a very musical family, it didn't always come easy—at times, it felt incredibly hard.

I took private trumpet lessons and worked diligently on my technique and tone. It wasn't always fun. It was challenging—sometimes even frustrating. On top of that, I battled fear. Performing in front of my peers brought pressure. Singing for family was one thing, but standing alone on stage was something else entirely. My mom wasn't right there beside me to cheer me on or tell everyone how great I was.

Through all the nerves and struggles, things began to come together. I eventually earned the position of first trumpet for most of my years in band, and I became a vocal soloist in choir. My hard work and perseverance paid off when I was awarded a music scholarship to Oregon State University.

Still, I had to walk through some difficult roads to get there. And that's the truth about growth—it often happens when things aren't easy, but when you choose to keep going anyway.

SURROUND YOURSELF

I am so blessed to have good people walking this winding road with me.

"You are the average of the five people you spend the most time with." —Jim Rohn

It's important to surround yourself with people who encourage you to keep moving with intention and purpose.

That's how a good life—and even a good business—comes together. Be clear about your purpose, your plans, and your goals.

CLEAR INTENTIONS

A life of purpose begins with clear intentions. And as you gain clarity, the winding road becomes a little easier to navigate.

And don't forget—enjoy the journey, even when the road is difficult.

I love what Frank Sinatra said: ***"I would like to be remembered as a man who had a wonderful time living life."***

Why not enjoy life?

Why not live your best life now?

The choice is up to you.

Whether you're struggling in your business, navigating personal challenges, or even celebrating a season when things are going great—choose to take that next step. Walk forward with intention toward your goals and dreams.

You can do it!

19 - SIGNIFICANCE... WHERE IT STARTS

There was a time when I believed significance came through success and possessions. I was convinced that if I landed a great job, worked hard, and made enough money, everything in life would fall into place. But I came to realize—that's not necessarily true.

Albert Einstein once said, ***"Try not to become a man of success, but rather try to become a man of value."***

This became evident to me in my first real job at Pihas, Schmidt, Westerdahl (PSW), when Leah and I were newly married. I worked tirelessly, running around the office so everyone could see how hard I was working. I wanted to prove myself.

I believed that if I worked hard enough, I would be promoted, earn more money, acquire more possessions, and life would be good.

I would be successful…Or so I thought.

SIGNIFICANCE

So, what is success—and what creates true significance in your life? This is a question we should all ask ourselves.

Life is a gift, full of opportunity and wonder. And we all strive for something. Many chase what the world calls success—measured by titles, accomplishments, and things: a better job, a bigger house, a nicer car, more stuff.

But is that really success?

Does it truly meet the deep need we all have—to live a life that matters?

"Each of you should use whatever gift you have received to serve others, as faithful stewards of God's grace in its various forms."
—1 Peter 4:10 (NIV)

Our perspective on life—and what is really important—drives much of what we see as significant.
There are many great voices out there, but John C. Maxwell is one of my favorites. He puts it best when he says:

"Success is mainly about myself… Significance is mainly about others. I've known many unfulfilled successful people, but everyone I know living a life of significance is fulfilled."

Significance doesn't start with success—it starts with purpose. And purpose begins when we stop asking, *"What can I get?"* and start asking, *"What can I give?"*

Bob Burg, author of *The Go-Giver*, says, **"Your true worth is determined by how much more you give in value than you take in payment."**

When we choose to live for something greater than ourselves, that's when life truly takes on meaning—and that's when we begin to make a real difference in the world!

THE JOURNEY

Like everything else in this life, discovering significance is a journey. Along the way, I've been blessed by people who made a lasting difference—people who saw value in me, believed in me, and chose to invest in my life.

Their encouragement, their time, even a few simple words—those moments mattered more than they ever realized.

THE POWER OF INFLUENCE

We all have those people—those who show up at just the right time and help shape who we become.

Who has been that kind of influence in your life?

Who has added value to your journey—perhaps without even knowing it?

For me, one of those people was Barbara Ellis, my journalism professor at Oregon State University.

When I was stuck, doubting myself, or didn't think I could finish something, she always had an encouraging word. Her belief in me inspired me to keep going—to keep writing, even when it felt impossible.

One of her favorite phrases has stuck with me ever since: *"Just do the next dumb thing."*

It may sound funny, but that simple statement carried wisdom. What she meant was—just keep going. Don't overthink. Don't freeze. Take the next step, even if it feels awkward or uncertain. It will work itself out if you keep moving forward.

Don't quit.

Don't give up.

To this day, when I face a challenge or get stuck in doubt, I still hear her voice:

"Just do the next dumb thing."

LIVING A LIFE THAT MATTERS

Significance that lasts a lifetime is created by someone who invests in others, is present, and truly cares.
Is that you?

Do you find both success and significance when you give?

Eleanor Roosevelt once said, *"For your own success to be real, it must contribute to the success of others."*

Giving to others is a key to a life of significant success. But it doesn't happen by accident—it's intentional.

As John C. Maxwell reminds us, *"Every person has a longing to be significant: to make a contribution; to be a part of something noble and purposeful."*

So today, take a step in that direction.

- Be the one who adds value.

- Lift others up.

- Speak life.

- Make a real difference.

Be a world changer in someone's life.

It starts with caring.

It grows through being present.

And it moves forward through positive, intentional action.

Start small. Maybe it's just a smile. Maybe it's a kind word.

As my friend Russ Johns always says: ***"Kindness is cool, and smiles are free!"***

Simple acts of kindness can shift someone's entire day—and maybe even their life.

Being a blessing is a choice. You can be significant today—if you choose to be.

Because in the end…

Significance isn't found in what you have—

It's found in who you choose to be.

20 - BE EXTRAORDINARY

Sometimes, going against conventional wisdom is exactly what it takes to create—or become—something extraordinary.

You've probably heard the old saying: ***"The definition of insanity is doing the same thing over and over again and expecting different results."*** That's more than just a clever quote—it's a real challenge to the way we live.

If you want something different, you have to do something different.

You have to take a chance.

You have to break the cycle.

I'll admit—I tend to get stuck in routines. Ironically, I've built those routines because I'm a right-brained, creative type. I've told you before, if it were entirely up to me, I'd fly by the seat of my pants and let the chips fall where they may. That might sound fun in theory, but in reality, I'd probably lose everything I own, forget every important appointment, and show up late to everything I do.

So, I've learned to create structure. Routines keep me grounded.

But here's the thing—routines, if you're not careful, can also keep you stuck.

If you want to live an extraordinary life, the kind that breaks through the noise and makes a difference, you have to ask yourself:

What does it really take to be extraordinary?

RISK

Are you willing to take a risk?

"If you want to do something extraordinary, there's always risk involved." —Felix Baumgartner

When you are willing to step out in faith, amazing things become possible. If you're willing to risk—

overcoming the fear that holds you back—God can lead you into life-changing opportunities.

So many wrestle with limiting beliefs and imposter syndrome, and those can stop you in your tracks. But remember: no one is perfect. God created you to connect, to build community, and to do life with people.

THE JOURNEY

Life is a journey, filled with ups and downs. But you get to choose whether you'll overcome the roadblocks and rise to do great things.

"The journey is never ending. There's always gonna be growth, improvement, adversity; you just gotta take it all in and do what's right, continue to grow, continue to live in the moment."
—Antonio Brown

Growth happens when we stay present and embrace the lessons hidden inside adversity. Even through pain and suffering.

"Suffering is an extraordinary teacher."
—Ryan Hall

Life is the greatest teacher, and hardship brings growth like nothing else can. It teaches lessons we may not want to learn, but that are necessary if we're to become who God created us to be.

True growth often comes through pain and adversity —things we would never have chosen but that shape us into more than we could imagine. We must embrace the journey and trust that good will come from it.

"And we know that in all things God works for the good of those who love Him, who have been called according to His purpose." —Romans 8:28

LIGHT

It's about believing there is Light in the darkness. And trusting that the Light is always stronger than the darkness.

This is what brings hope and inspiration in the hardest of times.

"Even when I walk through the darkest valley, I will not be afraid, for You are close beside me."
—Psalm 23:4

There is something greater than ourselves. A higher power. God gives us the strength to become extraordinary.

But let's be real—the world can feel overwhelming at times. So what do you do?

"There is a light in this world, a healing spirit more powerful than any darkness we may encounter. We sometimes lose sight of this force when there is suffering, too much pain. Then suddenly, the spirit will emerge through the lives of ordinary people who hear a call and answer in extraordinary ways." —Mother Teresa

Remember what Mother Teresa said. Remember that the Spirit of God can rise up within you and turn the ordinary into extraordinary.

You already have it in you. With God's help, you can use it.

Don't give your power away. Trust Him. You have more inside you than you realize. The choice is yours —use the talents you've been given.

Your life is navigated by you. And remember:

Life happens… and then you choose.

So choose courage over fear. Choose faith over doubt. Choose purpose over comfort. Because an extraordinary life doesn't just happen—it's built one bold decision at a time.

With God's strength and your willingness to step out, you can rise above ordinary and live a life of impact, meaning, and joy.

Don't settle for less. Step into the extraordinary—you were created for it.

21 - THE PROCESS OF BUILDING COMMUNITY

I learned early on the importance of community. I've always been a people person and naturally sought out opportunities to be with others. Whether it was through music or sports as a kid, I loved being around people and building relationships. I was determined to work with others to make a difference in whatever I took on.

I remember one project in particular from junior high. A group of us decided to put together a lip-sync performance to a popular band from the '70s for our school talent show. We worked hard, had a blast practicing, and when the big night came—we were a hit! Everyone loved it.

But what really stuck with me wasn't just the fun or the applause. It was the way working together on something creative brought us closer. We grew as friends, learned to depend on each other, and discovered how much joy comes from building something meaningful—together.

We were created for community—to grow together, encourage one another, and help each other become better. We are truly better together.

But let's be honest—coming together isn't always easy. Building real relationships takes time, patience, and grace. It's a process of showing up, being vulnerable, and committing to the long haul.

"As iron sharpens iron, so one person sharpens another." —Proverbs 27:17 (NIV)

When I first started in business, I tried to go it alone. I was in sales, and that world often breeds a me-against-you mentality. I was young and determined to make a name for myself. Nose to the grindstone, I pushed forward on my own.

The problem with that approach is simple: one person can only accomplish so much. But many people working together can accomplish so much more.

When I began networking and building community, I discovered incredible advantages. First of all, working with others was more fun—and far more productive.

Like I've said before: We are better together!

I started by getting involved with the local Chamber of Commerce, and from there, my circle grew. I met amazing people I could learn from, grow with, and serve—and they, in turn, connected me with others. I was amazed at how quickly opportunities and relationships blossomed.

When you build community, it fosters collaboration where everyone wins. It sharpens us in the process. We become a team—encouraging, supporting, and holding one another accountable.

THE PURPOSE OF SHARPENING

"Yes, we want to encourage each other, cheer each other on, and sharpen each other emotionally, physically, and spiritually. But when you truly think about the implications of such a description, this verse is anything but quaint."
—YouVersion

Sharpening one another means being present in both the good times and the hard ones. It takes intentionality. It takes purpose.

"Iron is sharpened through heat and friction, through cutting and slicing. As it is beaten, it is reshaped into something beautiful and purposeful—even better than before."
—YouVersion

That's the truth. Even when we feel beaten down or stretched thin, God can use those very moments to shape us—if we're willing. The process may be painful, but it is never pointless.

"Just as we develop our physical muscles through overcoming opposition—such as lifting weights—we develop our character muscles by overcoming challenges and adversity."
—Stephen R. Covey

STRONGER THROUGH RELATIONSHIPS

We grow through adversity. We develop depth through difficulty. And when we allow others to walk alongside us in that growth, we're not just becoming stronger—we're becoming sharper.

Sharpening done right is rooted in love and intention. It's not random or reckless—it's relational. We are shaped by those who care enough to help chip away the excess, the parts of us that don't reflect who God created us to be.

"Sharpening is purposeful, but it can also be painful. It's intentional friction that often results in a purer, stronger, sharper character. We aren't sharpened by thoughtless, careless, or unintentional relationships, but by those who lovingly help chip away the excess junk—who can recognize and visualize the masterpiece God wants us to become." —YouVersion

"We are not meant to go through life alone. We were created to depend on God and on each other." —Rick Warren

LIVING WITH PURPOSE AND INTENTION

Living with purpose—and on purpose—isn't always easy, but it's necessary. It's about removing distractions and clutter, and making space for the life God intended.

Seek out relationships that lift you up and speak truth into your life. Surround yourself with people who challenge you, encourage you, and remind you of your purpose.

"Unity is strength… when there is teamwork and collaboration, wonderful things can be achieved." —Mattie Stepanek

DON'T WALK ALONE

Community is a gift, but it's also a responsibility. God designed us to need each other. That's not weakness —that's wisdom. Don't isolate yourself or pull away from the very people who want to walk with you.

If you want to make a lasting impact—if you want to live a life of meaning—do it with others.

And remember:

"A friend is someone who knows the song in your heart and can sing it back to you when you have forgotten the words." —C.S. Lewis

"We rise by lifting others." —Robert Ingersoll

CHOOSE TO BUILD COMMUNITY

Every day, you have a choice: stay stuck or grow. Stay isolated or engage. Stay surface-level or go deeper.

This is your life.

Choose to build
Choose to grow
Choose community

Because when you choose connection, you don't just change your own life—you help change the world around you.

You were created for connection—and with God's help, you can thrive in it.

22 - COLLABORATION OVER ISOLATION

Are You Doing Life Alone?

Are you collaborating and working with others—or isolating yourself?

I have come to believe with all my heart that we are better together.

Trying to go it alone is often where we run into trouble. We were never meant to carry everything on our own.

"God doesn't intend for you to handle all the pain and stress in your life by yourself. We were wired for each other. We need each other."
—Rick Warren

We gain strength from others. We were created for community—to walk together, to encourage one another, and to share both the challenges and the good times.

Working with others brings joy, meaning, and connection into our lives.

"We need joy as we need air. We need love as we need water. We need each other as we need the earth we share." —Maya Angelou

Let me say it again: We need each other.

LESSONS FROM THE TEAM

As someone who loves sports, I believe there are powerful lessons found in the world of athletics. Teams thrive on collaboration. No great team wins on the back of one person alone.

I remember back in my early years of basketball, I would often try to take the ball one-on-one, convinced I could always beat my defender off the dribble and score. But I'll never forget the day my coach sat me down and had a serious talk with me about the concept of **TEAM**. In fact, he told me that if I didn't learn to pass the ball, I'd spend more time sitting on the bench than playing on the court.

That conversation was a turning point. I discovered that my team functioned so much better when I would drive and dish the ball to a teammate for a good shot. Not only did we win more games, but the joy of seeing us succeed together was far greater than anything I could accomplish on my own.

We really were **better together**—as a team, not just as individuals.

"Individual commitment to a group effort—that is what makes a team work, a company work, a society work, a civilization work."
—Vince Lombardi

When each of us does our part and commits to something bigger than ourselves, we multiply our opportunities and impact. Collaboration is the key to success.

Have I mentioned yet that **we are better together?**

COMING TOGETHER TAKES EFFORT

We need to come together—and stay together. That is how we find lasting growth and true success.

"Coming together is a beginning. Keeping together is progress. Working together is success." —Henry Ford

It takes effort to stay connected. But with the right perspective and an intentional heart, collaboration becomes powerful and fulfilling.

With focus, perseverance, and the right people around you, you can accomplish incredible things.

"I'm not the smartest fellow in the world, but I sure can pick smart colleagues."
—Franklin D. Roosevelt

CHOOSE YOUR CIRCLE WISELY

Choose wisely who you walk with. When you surround yourself with great people, you become better.

As I have said previously, *"You are the average of the five people you spend the most time with."*
—Jim Rohn

So… who are you in community with?

You should never be the smartest person in the room. Surround yourself with those who stretch you, inspire you, and challenge you. Not to copy them— but to grow from their example. Be authentic, but let their lives be a springboard to your future.

"Surround yourself only with people who are going to lift you higher." —Oprah Winfrey

When you are intentional about this, the impact on your life and success can be dramatic. It's not about ego—it's about growth.

THE POWER OF UNITY

"If everyone is moving forward together, then success takes care of itself." —Henry Ford

That's the truth. You can achieve some success alone, but it's teamwork that truly makes the dream work. Coming together brings collaboration, fresh ideas, and the unique talents each person carries.

When you isolate yourself and try to achieve your goals alone, it often leaves you feeling empty. It robs you of the fulfillment that comes from truly making a difference in the lives of others. And that is no way to live.

So why not be wise—and work as a team?

All truly successful people have learned this formula, and it has made all the difference.

"Talent wins games, but teamwork and intelligence win championships."
—Michael Jordan

You can be a champion in whatever you do—if you intentionally focus your energy, surround yourself with the right people, and collaborate with heart and humility.

It's not about what *you* can do alone—it's about what *we* can accomplish together. That's where the real impact is made.

Don't go it alone.

Don't isolate yourself.

"Alone we can do so little; together we can do so much." —Helen Keller

THE CHOICE IS YOURS

You don't have to do life alone. Collaboration opens doors, expands possibilities, and deepens your purpose.

Choose connection. Choose community. Choose collaboration.

The choice is yours—step into it today.

23 - BE STILL

I am definitely someone who likes to stay busy. I've always moved quickly from task to task and often taken on more than I probably should.

I remember my dad often telling me to slow down and take a moment to think things through. But I was always push, push, push—wanting to get as much done as fast as I could... then rushing off to the next thing.

There were times this drive helped me, but more often it led to sloppiness and mistakes. Sometimes accidents happened. Other times, I jumped into things too quickly without considering what was truly best for me in the long run.

I've learned that sometimes it's best to slow down and be still.

The challenge is, we lead busy lives. We're constantly on the move, and in the process, we often lose sight of our true purpose.

So let me ask you—why did you get up this morning?

Purpose is essential. To find the direction you need and align with your true calling, you must sometimes pause—be still—and recognize that there are forces bigger than yourself at work.

I love Psalm 46:10, which says: ***"Be still, and know that I am God."***

As a man of faith, I trust God and know there are moments when I just have to let go and let Him do His work. He is the One who aligns my purpose in life.

LIVING WITH PURPOSE

How about you?

Are you focused on your purpose?

Are you trying to go it alone—or are you trusting in something bigger than yourself?

If you have a pulse, you still have a purpose. God has created you with hope and a future.

"For I know the plans I have for you," declares the Lord, *"plans to prosper you and not to harm you, plans to give you hope and a future."*
—Jeremiah 29:11 (NIV)

We are all works in progress. But taking time—being still—is essential if you want to stay on the right path. Stillness gives you time to process, to reflect, and to make space for creativity and productivity.

It's not always easy. That's why I love this quote by Kirk Franklin: *"Now everyday ain't gonna be perfect, but it still don't mean today don't have purpose."*

In the midst of life's imperfections, you still have a job to do. But it starts with you—by giving yourself space to align with your purpose.

Alignment is critical. When you get distracted or drift off course, the consequences are rarely good. That's why it's so important to live within your purpose and intentionally keep moving in the right direction.

PASSION AND CALLING

You don't have to be pushed into your purpose—it's God-given.

"If you have a strong purpose in life, you don't have to be pushed. Your passion will drive you there." —Roy T. Bennett

When you're passionate about something, that's usually a good sign you're walking in the direction God designed for you.

It is always better to work within the strengths He gave you and the passion He planted deep within you. That's what produces the results He intended when He created you.

So, keep going.

"When you walk in your purpose, you inspire others to find theirs." —Unknown

This is where true impact happens—when your life not only fulfills your calling but also inspires others to step into theirs. Inspiration is a blessing that fuels both you and those around you.

But remember—staying aligned requires stillness. Take the time to listen, reflect, and allow God to guide your steps.

THE POWER OF STILLNESS

I love the stillness of a quiet morning. I love the peace and calm of the outdoors.

As I talked about earlier, when I was young, my family lived on five acres of forest.. I remember going out to explore, surrounded by the beauty of God's creation. I appreciated the stillness—the way it was both exciting and rejuvenating at the same time.

"Learning how to be still, to really be still and let life happen—that stillness becomes a radiance."
—Morgan Freeman

When you practice stillness, you begin to radiate purpose. That radiance brings significance not only to your life but also to the lives of those around you.

"Within stillness, we find the strength to move forward with clarity and peace." —Unknown

Choosing stillness each morning isn't just a nice idea —it's a game changer. It clears your mind, centers your heart, and aligns your steps with the purpose God designed for you. In the quiet, He speaks. In the stillness, He shapes you. And even in the midst of the chaos of life His inner stillness keeps you steady, focused, and unshakable.

So today… stop. Breathe. Be still. Listen to the still small voice of God guiding you. Let Him direct your steps, strengthen your heart, and fuel your purpose. The life you've been waiting for—the extraordinary, impactful, God-honoring life—is waiting for you. Step into it boldly. Step into it now.

"Be still, and know that I am God!" —Psalm 46:10

"Stillness is where clarity begins." —Unknown

24 - NAVIGATING THIS MESSY LIFE

"Life is a blessed mess, and we're all just trying to navigate through it." —Unknown

It's true—life can be messy, unpredictable, and full of challenges. But even in the middle of the mess, you are blessed. Sometimes, it's just harder to see because of everything going on around you.

MY FAITHFUL BEAGLE

Today, as I write this, I've just returned from the vet after losing my faithful beagle. She was just a couple of months shy of 14 years old. Her name was Maddie, and she was one of the most loyal companions I've ever had.

Maddie was always by my side. She walked with me every morning, slept in my office while I worked, and never failed to bring me comfort. Her loyalty and sweet spirit were constant reminders of God's goodness.

She was faithful until the end, and letting her go was one of the hardest things I've ever had to do. I'm still coming to grips with the fact that she won't be there waiting for me tomorrow morning.

It was difficult watching her body begin to fail. We had just returned from a family vacation in Maine when she started to decline. Through it all, God has been with me. I choose to remember the joy, the love, and the companionship Maddie brought into my life. That was a gift from God—and a part of how I choose to navigate this messy life.

When life is painful, I look to Jesus, who gives me *"the peace that surpasses all understanding"* —Philippians 4:7

A MATTER OF PERSPECTIVE

Perspective is everything. The way you choose to see your circumstances shapes how you experience them. Navigation begins with a good perspective and a positive attitude, no matter what challenges you're facing.

As Chip Ingram says: *"Living above my circumstances occurs when my perspective interprets my circumstances, rather than my circumstances determining my perspective."*

That quote has carried me through many tough moments.

PERSPECTIVE ON CANCER

At the beginning of my cancer journey, my oncologist told me the number one factor in how well I would fight and recover was my perspective and attitude. That stuck with me.

We often underestimate just how much our thinking influences our health and our life.

A positive perspective doesn't mean denying the hard things. It means choosing to walk through them with faith, gratitude, and the willingness to receive help along the way.

"The Lord is my strength and my song; He has given me victory." —Psalm 118:14

And that's exactly what He has been for me.

GOD AND COMMUNITY

God and community give us strength.

Jesus meets us in the mess of life! He is faithful and can guide us through any circumstance. Community, too, helps us navigate life's challenges.

Whatever you believe, hold onto hope as you travel this journey we call life.

"Life is a journey, not a destination."
—Ralph Waldo Emerson

Along the way, we grow stronger if we stay present and pay attention. But growth also comes with risk. You have to step out, take chances, and navigate the path you were created for.

"Everything in life has some risk, and what you actually have to learn to do is how to navigate it."
—Reid Hoffman

As you learn, you gain wisdom to share with others. And when you help others through their own challenges, you not only strengthen them—you strengthen yourself.

As John C. Maxwell reminds us: *"Sometimes you win… sometimes you learn."*

Life doesn't always go the way we plan. It can get real messy, no matter what we do.

EMBRACING THE MESS

So, where do you go from here?

If you're in the middle of the mess, start by checking your perspective. How are you looking at your life's journey?

I came across a coach named Krista online who said something powerful: *"A beautiful and meaningful life is messy!"*

She's right. You can't avoid the mess entirely, but your perspective and how you deal with it make all the difference.

"What if we accept that it's all messy, stop looking for perfect, and embrace what is."
—Krista

And there it is—embrace what is, and move forward in spite of your messy circumstances.

CHOOSE HOPE, CHOOSE STRENGTH

Remember: *"Life happens… and then you choose!"*

You can overcome the mess of life by choosing a good perspective and a resilient mindset.

This messy life is worth the fight. Hold onto hope. Stay strong. And keep believing—because there are awesome days ahead.

The life you live is the life you choose.

So get out there—don't let the mess hold you back. Rise above it. Live with faith. Step boldly into your purpose. Claim your best life now—and make the impact you were created for!

25 - WHAT NEXT?

By now, you've probably heard it countless times:
Life happens—and then you choose!

So, what should you do next?

"In any moment of decision, the best thing you can do is the right thing, the next best thing is the wrong thing, and the worst thing you can do is nothing." —Theodore Roosevelt

Staying still, frozen by fear, is a losing battle no matter how you look at it. Life will move on with or without your participation. But you were created with the ability to do something special—and now is your moment. Now is your time.

KEEP MOVING FORWARD

Worry and fear can slow you down—or stop you completely. That's why you must shift your focus from the impossible to the possible.

Ask yourself: *What can I do now? Where am I headed? What is the purpose driving me toward my goals?*

"Don't dwell on what went wrong. Instead, focus on what to do next. Spend your energies moving forward toward finding the answer."
—Denis Waitley

Your energy is limited, so use it wisely. Make a plan —and do it now! Waiting only works against you, feeding doubt and second-guessing.

"A good plan violently executed now is better than a perfect plan executed next week."
—George S. Patton

Even small, consistent steps keep you moving forward. You don't need giant leaps every time— steady progress is what truly gets you there.

Momentum is built one step at a time. Keep moving. Keep pressing on. Let the gears of progress turn.

THINK POSITIVELY

Negativity is a weight you don't need to carry. You get to choose how you respond after life happens. Either you set your mindset—or it will be set for you.

"Every positive thought is a silent prayer that will change your life." —Unknown

You become what you think about. Choose positive, faith-filled thoughts. I've been blessed by God with the ability to turn negative thoughts into hopeful ones, and I practice it daily.

And yes—have fun along the way! Life isn't meant to be all serious and stressful.

"There are really just two options: positive or negative. And the alternative to positive is not where you want to go."

"I just look at what's the most fun thing I can do next. I'm not looking to prove anything, or break away. I feel so lucky, honestly, that I'm still working." —Lucy Lawless

Enjoy your life. Be grateful for the blessings God has given you. Keep moving forward, even when challenges try to pull you down.

WHEN YOU FEEL STUCK

We all face moments when we feel stuck, unsure, or afraid to move forward. I remember the advice of my Oregon State journalism professor, Barbara Ellis:

"Just do the next dumb thing!"

Her words are simple, but they carry powerful wisdom. Don't overthink. Don't stop. Don't let fear kill your goals and dreams. Keep moving—one step at a time—and make forward progress.

TRUST GOD AND TAKE ACTION

Stay positive. Keep moving. Trust God's timing. Live your life with intention, faith, and joy.

"Commit to the Lord whatever you do, and He will establish your plans." —Proverbs 16:3 (NIV)

Life happens. The choice is yours. So choose faith. Choose joy. Choose action. Don't wait for the perfect moment—God is already at work in your life. Step boldly into the journey He has prepared for you.

Rise above fear. Rise above doubt. Keep moving forward, trusting that God will guide every step. This is your moment. This is your life. And it's up to you to live it fully, intentionally, and courageously.

CONCLUSION

I am just an ordinary person, like you, doing my best to navigate this life each day. Yet even in the ordinary, there is extraordinary potential—because God has created you with purpose, influence, and the ability to make a difference.

So, where do you want to go next? What do you want to accomplish—not just in your career, your finances, or your personal achievements—but in your life as a whole?

You have impact on others every single day, whether you realize it or not. But influence is a choice. Are you going to choose to be a positive force today—for yourself, for those around you, and for the world—or will you let life and circumstances shape you into someone you never intended to be?

It's up to you.

THE POWER OF CHOICE

Life happens. That is true. But what is even more true is that *you always have the power to choose your response.*

"Your life does not get better by chance, it gets better by change." —Jim Rohn

Every choice you make—every decision, every action—has a ripple effect. You can let fear, doubt, or the chaos of life paralyze you, or you can step forward in faith, with courage and purpose. You can choose to move toward your goals, your passions, and your calling, even when the path seems uncertain.

It doesn't require perfection. It requires commitment. It doesn't require giant leaps. It requires consistent steps in the right direction. And when you act with intention, you open the door for God's guidance, wisdom, and blessing to move in your life.

EMBRACE YOUR PURPOSE

You were created for more than just going through the motions. You were created for purpose. For impact. For connection. For love. When you align your life with that purpose, you not only experience fulfillment—you inspire others to do the same.

"Go confidently in the direction of your dreams. Live the life you have imagined."
—Henry David Thoreau

Your passions, your gifts, and your influence are not accidents. They are part of God's plan. When you choose to live intentionally—investing in others, nurturing relationships, and walking in faith—you step into a life that matters, a life that leaves a legacy, and a life that reflects the love and goodness of God.

STEP INTO ACTION

Now is the time. Don't wait for the perfect moment. Don't wait until fear is gone. Don't wait for all the circumstances to align. Step forward now. Take that next step, even if it feels small or uncertain. Momentum begins with action.

"Small steps in the right direction are better than standing still." —Unknown

Every choice counts. Every action matters. Every day is an opportunity to live intentionally, to lift others up, and to leave a positive mark on the world around you. You have been given a life that matters. You have been given a purpose that is uniquely yours. And you have been given the freedom—and the responsibility—to choose how you will live it.

YOUR MOMENT

So, what will you do today? Choose faith. Choose courage. Choose joy. Choose love. Step boldly into the life God has designed for you. Be a light. Be a blessing. Be a positive force in a world that so desperately needs it.

Life happens… and then you choose!

Now, go get it. Your life, your purpose, and your moment are waiting.

Live Your Best Life Now!

https://www.russhedge.com